How Is It With Your Soul?

How Is It With Your Soul?

Class Leader's Manual for Use With *This Day*

Denise L. Stringer

ABINGDON PRESS / Nashville

HOW IS IT WITH YOUR SOUL? CLASS LEADER'S MANUAL FOR USE WITH *THIS DAY*

Copyright © 2004 by Abingdon Press

This book is printed on acid-free paper.

ISBN 0-687-06697-2

All Scripture quotations unless noted otherwise are taken from the *New Revised Standard Version of the Bible,* copyright © 1989, by the Division of Christian Education of the National Council of the Churches of Christ in the United States of America. Used by permission. All rights reserved.

Scripture quotations marked RSV are taken from the *Revised Standard Version of the Bible,* copyright 1946, 1952, 1971 by the Division of Christian Education of the National Council of the Churches of Christ in the United States of America. Used by permission. All rights reserved.

The first prayer on page 54 is from A Service of Word and Table I © 1972, 1980, 1985, 1989 The United Methodist Publishing House. Used by permission.

Prayer on page 56 is from *United Methodist Book of Worship* © 1992 by United Methodist Publishing House. Used by permission.

04 05 06 07 08 09 10 11 12 13—10 9 8 7 6 5 4 3 2 1

MANUFACTURED IN THE UNITED STATES OF AMERICA

Contents

Foreword

How is it with your soul? There is no more important and no more central question for Christians. Our relationship to God is always the first question and the first priority as we seek to fashion a faithful discipleship. Denise Stringer begins where our Wesleyan heritage begins, with God and the individual's relationship with God. From there she skillfully translates into twenty-first century language and structure the heart of the Wesleyan movement's organization and practice.

Denise Stringer is a biblical scholar, writer, and pastor who understands that the future of the church has always depended upon faithful lay leaders. Laypersons assume leadership roles in the church and practice their discipleship in faithful ways in every setting into which their lives take them. In this *Class Leader's* manual, she offers a solid theological foundation and a step-by-step process to form, conduct, and sustain an effective small group movement in the congregation—a movement that will result in the formation of men and women in the image of Christ.

This movement is for and by laity. While there are clear pastoral duties involved, the bulk of this ministry is in the hands of laypersons in the congregation. The formation of Christian disciples has always been the work of the Holy Spirit, but creating the setting and nurturing the birthing of the new person in Christ has often been the work of laity. Clergy have their part, but if there is to be a restoration of the vitality and missionary thrust of Methodism, it must be carried out by laypersons. This is true in order to reach large numbers of people and it is also true because of the commission given to every Christian at baptism. The commission to winsome and faithful witness and mission comes to all, but only the well equipped will be prepared to fulfill their calling.

How Is It With Your Soul? is rooted in Scripture and tradition and yet is written in language and images that appeal to the twenty-first century disciple of Jesus Christ, language and images that laity understand and can readily translate into daily living. However, this resource is not prepared for those who wish simply to gloss over the demands of the gospel or give up the rewards of faithfulness. It is designed to lead the user toward a way of life that is enriching and sustainable for a lifetime.

The goal of this resource is to prepare every faith community to reach out to meet people where they are, relate them to God, nurture them in faith, care for them as whole persons, and equip them for effective ministries beyond the walls of the church. In other words, it is about the formation of disciples into the image of God in Christ and sending them into the world as faithful disciples. And it all begins with God. How is it with your soul?

Rueben P. Job

Introduction

"Looking to Jesus the pioneer and perfecter of our faith."
—Hebrews 12:2a

From the beginning, the Methodist movement has sought to lead people beyond nominal Christianity into a vital relationship with God (Romans 3:22). The practice of faithfulness in the Wesleyan tradition focuses on the knowledge of God in Christ Jesus, seeking the mind of Christ, or "the renewal of the soul after the image of God, in righteousness and true holiness" ("Thoughts Upon Methodism," John Wesley, *Arminian Magazine*, 1787, found in *Selections from the Writings of the Rev. John Wesley, M.A.*, p. 205). John and Charles Wesley, the founders of Methodism, believed that personal conversion, when properly nurtured within the *Class Meeting*, would lead to lifelong Christian discipleship and the spread of scriptural holiness across the land. *How Is It With Your Soul?* has been designed to equip clergy and laity to renew the original vision and methodology of the Wesleyan movement for the twenty-first century.

This manual for *Class Leaders* is intended for use in conjunction with *This Day: A Wesleyan Way of Prayer*, primarily within the adult education program of the local church. These resources, when employed as foundational components of the local church's discipleship system, will support spiritual formation over the life span of the class. A revival of the *Class Meeting* system, accompanied by daily prayer and reading of Scripture, will help to fill the gap that has been created by the historic division between the Church of England and American Methodism, as well as address the widespread decline in spiritual vitality within the Methodist movement. The material has been developed with a clear focus on the contemporary ministry setting, as well as with a strong desire to base current practice on the original Wesleyan methodology. The best of the many sciences that can inform and strengthen the mission of the Church in the postmodern world have been accessed in this effort to support twenty-first century *Class Leaders* in providing lay pastoral oversight for the people called Methodists.

The way of life to which the followers of Jesus believe themselves called may best be described by using Jesus' own words: the losing of one's life to find it (Mark 8:35) or taking up the cross daily (Luke 14:27). This way is neither the ascetic's practice of self-denial nor a heavy burden of rules or religious practices (Matthew 11:30; Galatians 5:1). It is nothing more and nothing less than a love for God that engages the whole person and every aspect of one's relationships with others.

John Wesley, the founder of Methodism, described the way of life he sought for his fellow Methodists when he wrote:

> A Methodist is one who has "the love of God shed abroad in his heart by the Holy Ghost given unto him;" one who "loves the Lord his God with all his heart, and with all his soul, and with all his mind, and with all his strength." God is the joy of his heart, and the desire of his soul; which is constantly crying out, "Whom have I in heaven but thee? And there is none upon earth that I desire beside thee! My God and my all! Thou art the strength of my heart, and my portion for ever!" (John Wesley, "The Character of a Methodist," in *Selections from the Writings of the Rev. John Wesley, MA,* arranged by Bishop Herbert Welch (Nashille: Abingdon Press, 1942), p. 295)

Using the Historic Wesleyan Plan for Spiritual Formation

From the beginning, John Wesley expected those who received the gospel to demonstrate a wholly Christian character. In his tract, *A Farther Appeal to Men of Reason and Religion*, John Wesley wrote, "I will not quarrel with you about any opinion. Only see that your heart be right toward God, that you know and love the Lord Jesus Christ; that you love your neighbour and walk as your Master walked; and I desire no more" (Part iii, 1745, in *Selections from the Writings of the Rev. John Wesley, MA*, p. 293).

There was no room in his movement for "almost Christians." All around him he saw parishes where the bulk of the members called themselves Christians but did not demonstrate the character of a truly converted life. He reviewed what he saw with a special concern for the quality of fellowship within the churches and asked, "Are not the bulk of the parishioners a mere rope of sand? What Christian connection is there between them? What intercourse in spiritual things? What watching over each other's souls?" ("The Almost Christian," *John Wesley's Fifty-Three Sermons*, ed. Edward H. Sugden, [Nashville: Abingdon Press, 1983], pp. 29-38).

Having proclaimed the gospel to thousands and seen hundreds of conversions, Wesley began to recognize the need to organize a means of nurturing Christian discipleship. The parish churches were wholly unfit to care for the souls of newly regenerate believers. Their clergy tended to undermine the converting experience of saving grace, to which George Whitefield's and the Wesleys' followers testified. They often excluded Methodists from the Lord's Table.

As the concerns grew and the need for oversight became more clear, Wesley and his colleagues began to organize new converts into classes or groups of twelve. *Class Leaders* functioned as *lay assistants* who watched over other souls living near one another.

Wesley wrote:

> No clergyman would assist at all. The expedient that remained was to
> find some one among themselves, who was upright of heart, and of
> sound judgment in the things of God; and to desire him to meet the rest
> as often as he could, in order to confirm them, as he was able, in the ways
> of God, either by reading to them, or by prayer, or by exhortation. God
> immediately gave a blessing hereto. In several places, by means of these
> plain men, not only those who had already begun to run well were hin-
> dered from drawing back to perdition; but other sinners also, from time
> to time, were converted from the error of their ways. (*Selections from the
> Writings of the Rev. John Wesley*, p. 189)

This model had been profitably used in the dissenting churches during
the English Reformation and would work well in the midst of the current
revival.

John and Charles Wesley first practiced the "method" of Methodism
while studying at Oxford. There they formed the Holy Club with George
Whitefield and others. These young men "earnestly desired to flee from
the wrath to come" and determined to practice the faith of Jesus by way
of regular visitation of the poor, the orphaned, the widows, and the
imprisoned. They met frequently, sometimes for up to three hours, to
search the Scriptures, pray, discuss the faith, and account for their work as
emissaries of mercy and as witnesses to the gospel among those in need.
Later, under the evangelical preaching of George Whitefield, John Wesley
took on the challenge of organizing new converts into classes and societies for the purpose of seeing that the fruit of evangelical conversion
matured into lifelong holiness.

Wesley's method for nurturing Christian discipleship became known as
the *Class Meeting* system. Its purpose was to provide for the nurture of the
members of the Methodist societies. All members in good standing would
"continue to evidence their desire of salvation, *First:* By doing no harm,
by avoiding evil of every kind; *Secondly:* By . . . doing good of every possible sort, and, as far as possible, to all; *Thirdly:* By attending upon all the
ordinances of God" ("The Methodist Societies: The Nature, Design and
General Rules of the United Societies" vol. 9 in *The Works of John Wesley*,
ed. Rupert E. Davies [Nashville: Abingdon Press, 1989], pp. 70-73). Wesley
admonished those who were charged with oversight of souls and the
maintenance of discipline according to the standard of the *General Rules*:

> If there be any among us who observe them not, who habitually break any
> of them, let it be known unto them who watch over that soul as they who
> must give an account. We will admonish him of the error of his ways. We
> will bear with him for a season. But then, if he repent not, he hath no more

place among us. We have delivered our own souls. (*The Book of Discipline* [Nashville: United Methodist Publishing House, 2000], ¶103, p. 74)

Methodists were to hold each other accountable on a weekly basis through lifelong participation in a *Class Meeting*. The *Class Meeting* provided a fellowship for mutual support, discipline, and edification. Its members were those who "having the *form* and seeking the *power* of godliness, united in order to pray together, to receive the word of exhortation, and to watch over one another in love, that they may help each other to work out their salvation." (*The Book of Discipline*, ¶103, p. 72)

Following John Wesley's design, classes convened once a week. Everyone was to arrive exactly at the stated hour, apart from some extraordinary reason. The session began at the appointed time with singing or prayer.

According to rules "drawn up" December 25, 1738, each member speaks "freely and plainly, the true state of our souls, with the faults we have committed in thought, word, or deed, and the temptations we have felt, since our last meeting." The leader initiates the sharing and then asks the rest, in order, "as many and as searching questions as may be, concerning their state, sins and temptations" (*The Early Methodist Class Meeting*, Appendix E, p. 200 or from *The Works of John Wesley*, 14 Vols. [London: Wesleyan Conference Office, 1872; reprinted, Grand Rapids, Michigan: Baker Book House, 1979], 8:272-73). The leader reports to the *ministers* and stewards of the *society* or congregation.

This method, sometimes referred to as *Christian Conferencing*, in conjunction with practicing "the ordinances of God," would serve to preserve the faithfulness of the converted and guide them toward "perfection in love." The *ordinances of God* that the Methodists were to practice were proven means of maintaining a right relationship with God. Jesus both practiced them himself and taught his disciples to do so. Methodists often refer to them as "the means of grace." Wesley composed a simple list of the spiritual practices that he expected of his fellow Methodists and published them as a part of the *General Rules* that were to govern the Methodist societies and guide the *Class Meetings* (*The Book of Discipline*, ¶103, p. 74). They are:

- The public worship of God

- The ministry of the Word, either read or expounded

- The Supper of the Lord

- Family and private prayer

- Searching the Scriptures

- Fasting or abstinence

Spiritual Formation Among Methodists Today

Early Methodists believed that to participate in a *Class Meeting* and keep the *General Rules* was to exercise due diligence lest their eternal soul be lost in judgment at the last day and their conversion be in vain. While contemporary Methodists experience less fear in the face of God than did their forebears, many recognize that to revert to the way of life they formerly followed or the lifestyle that the *society* at large practices will lead to spiritual emptiness, if not to the ruin of all that matters most in life. Therefore, contemporary Methodists seek a pattern of mutual encouragement and guidance and a means of growing daily in faith and faithfulness. *How Is It With Your Soul?* provides a discipleship system in the Wesleyan tradition that incorporates a daily structure for prayer and the study of Scripture, as well as regular *Class Meetings*, in order that the character of Christian discipleship may once more become both apparent and regularly practiced among the people called Methodists.

All members of the class shall also be active members of a local church where they worship regularly, partake of the Sacrament of Holy Communion whenever it is offered, contribute to the financial support of the ministry, and seek to live a godly life both in private and in public. *Class Leaders* hold themselves accountable to the *director* (coordinator of *Class Leaders*) or *minister* in charge. Class sessions include prayer, a means of mutual accountability and support, and study. The purpose of this method of spiritual formation is to nurture communion with God and the development of Christian character within the community of God's people.

A holistic practice of the Christian faith requires solitude, community, and servanthood. The disciple of Christ engages in a covenant with God and neighbor, especially "those of the household of faith or groaning so to be" (*The Book of Discipline*, ¶103, p. 73; Galatians 6:10). This is no solitary life. Rather, it is a faith that manifests itself in love, both within the congregation and in the world. When we practice this way of life, we live out our mission to "save persons, heal relationships, transform social structures, and spread scriptural holiness, thereby changing the world" (*The Book of Discipline*, ¶121, p. 88).

Our Mission: Addressing the Human Condition

To say that we are in the business of saving people is to point to something the early church fathers called "the cure of souls." Human beings suffer from a state of moral and spiritual corruption (Romans 1:21). The teaching of the Church tells us that "man is very far gone from original

4

righteousness, and of his own nature inclined to evil, and that continually" (*Of Original or Birth Sin, Articles of Religion*). Moreover, the human condition "is such that he cannot turn and prepare himself, by his own natural strength and works, to faith, and calling upon God; wherefore we have no power to do good works, pleasant and acceptable to God, without the *grace* of God by Christ preventing us, that we may have a good will, and working with us, when we have that good will" (*Of Free Will, Articles of Religion*). Thus, apart from God's leading us to receive the revelation of God in Jesus by faith and our practicing the means of *grace*, we are without hope of living whole and holy lives. The method of Methodism takes as its first task, then, bringing the believer into a relationship with God, so that the goodness of God may transform the believer's mind and conform his or her entire being to the mind of Christ (Philippians 2:5; Romans 12:2). The church does this by proclaiming the gospel and encouraging others to respond (Mark 1:15; Romans 10:8-11, 14-15). With faith and repentance come new birth and an ongoing process of sanctification (1 Thessalonians 4:3-8; Romans 6:17-19).

> We believe sanctification is the work of God's grace through the Word and the Spirit, by which those who have been born again are cleansed from sin in their thoughts, words and acts, and are enabled to live in accordance with God's will, and to strive for holiness without which no one will see the Lord.
>
> Entire sanctification is a state of perfect love, righteousness and true holiness which every regenerate believer may obtain by being delivered from the power of sin, by loving God with all the heart, soul, mind and strength, and by loving one's neighbor as one's self.... The Christian must continue on guard against spiritual pride and seek to gain victory over every temptation to sin. He must respond wholly to the will of God so that sin will lose its power over him; and the world, the flesh, and the devil are put under his feet. Thus he rules over these enemies with watchfulness through the power of the Holy Spirit. (*Sanctification, Articles of Religion*, see *The United Methodist Book of Discipline*, ¶ 103, p. 70)

Thus, the daily practice of prayer and regular participation in a *Class Meeting* support both the individual and the church in the pursuit of holy living and faithfulness in mission to the world.

Focusing Accountability: "How Is It With Your Soul?"

When the class gathers, the leader may ask the members the question, "How is it with your soul?" or otherwise inquire after the members' faithfulness during a time of *reflection.* John Wesley frequently inquired after the souls of those with whom he corresponded and often spoke of the state of the soul in its relationship with God. He might ask, "How do you find your soul?" or "Do you find your soul as much alive to God as ever?" (A Letter to Mrs. Mortimer, John Wesley, 1777). Never was the question intended as an invitation to become introspective, as if absorbed in self-examination. The pastoral question sought to lift the inmost thoughts of the believer toward God.

When the question is asked in the context of a *Class Meeting,* it is as if Jesus himself were watching over the believers through the supportive fellowship of the class. By asking the question, the *Class Leader* holds up a mirror to the souls under his or her care. Class members respond as if speaking to their Master Teacher and Lord, while allowing their fellow disciples to overhear them and encourage them.

Members share what they feel comfortable revealing about their inmost selves, their conscious love for God, and their conscience with regard to love for their neighbors. Participants hold each other accountable for living humbly and simply in conformity with the teachings of Jesus and for seeking forgiveness and peace with God and neighbor (Matthew 5:3–7:27). The objective standard by which they give an account of themselves includes the regular practice of the means of grace, as guided by *This Day: A Wesleyan Way of Prayer,* and faithfulness to scriptural holiness as summarized in the *General Rules.*

Daily Prayer

The guide to daily prayer includes two primary components: (1) *forms of prayer* in the Wesleyan tradition (a *daily office*); and (2) a lectionary of Scripture readings for use every day. The discipline of integrating these elements into a regular personal practice, including a definite time and place for relating directly to God, will provide for sound and ongoing spiritual nurture.

The *daily office* and collects for the day come from the tradition of the church, especially the *Book of Common Prayer.* The language has been modernized with an eye and ear for preserving the original beauty and syntax. Regular use of the *daily office* will serve as a bridge over which the believer can pass toward communion with God, as an invitation to take and eat the bread of God's Word, as a setting in which the believer can attend to the things that matter most, and as a tool for ministry with others.

The reading of Scripture as guided by the daily lectionary invites Methodists to listen prayerfully for the voice of God. *This Day: A Wesleyan*

Way of Prayer provides for praying a psalm each day of the month, as well as reading two other passages, one from the Hebrew Scriptures and one from either the Gospels or other New Testament writings (for example, the *Epistles*). Over the course of two years, those who follow the daily lectionary will have prayed through the major sections and most treasured passages of the Bible. The goal of spreading scriptural holiness requires that every Methodist be steeped in the Scripture. This habit of daily listening for the Word of God through a disciplined reading of the Old and New Testaments will help create a lifelong pattern of biblical faithfulness (Matthew 6:33).

The prayer book *This Day: A Wesleyan Way of Prayer* offers *Class Leaders*, as well as class members, model prayers for use in a wide variety of settings and in response to particular needs. Laity can use the book in family devotions, at mealtime, in small groups at the noon hour or at other breaks in the work day, in visitation of the sick and elderly, during meetings, as well as in private prayer. All who use the book will find their prayer life informed and enriched by the variety of gifts and faith perspectives this rich tradition of prayer represents. Those who feel that they "do not know how to pray as [they] ought" (Romans 8:26b) will find guidance and encouragement in the patterns of prayer and structure for daily devotional life by which the church has found edification and inspiration over the centuries.

Perceiving Spiritual Formation Through a Biblical Lens

Valuing the historic roots of Methodism orients the people called Methodists and gives us a sense of mandate. John Wesley's approach to spiritual formation was, however, nothing other than an attempt to live "according to the method laid down in the Bible" (Note to *The Complete English Dictionary*, 1753 found in Welch, p. 295). He wrote in his *Preface to Explanatory Notes upon the New Testament*:

> Would to God that all the party names, and unscriptural phrases and forms, which have divided the Christian world, were forgot; and that we might all agree to sit down together, as humble, loving disciples, at the feet of our common Master, to hear his word, to imbibe his Spirit, and to transcribe his life in our own! (1755, Works, vii, 536, in *Selections from the Writings of Mr. John Wesley, M.A.*, p. 292)

Thinking in terms of biblical images and stories may do more than anything else to help us visualize what we are hoping to achieve as twenty-first century disciples of Jesus. Participants and *Class Leaders* can identify with the first disciples when they read Matthew 5:1-2: "When Jesus saw the crowds, he went up the mountain; and after he sat down, his disciples came to him. Then he began to speak, and taught them, saying . . . "

Jesus regularly sought rest and solitude for personal refreshment. He often took his closest friends with him. As if on retreat from their active ministry, Jesus and his disciples took time to sit together while Jesus shared his heart and his deepest understanding of God and God's work in the world.

Alone with Jesus, the disciples began to see through Jesus' eyes. They developed a profound devotion to the kingdom of God in the midst of them. They found themselves being formed into fellow workers with Christ. It can be so among the people called Methodists when, in the twenty-first century, they gather in small groups, as in a community of divine love, to listen for the Word of God through prayer, the reading and study of the Scriptures, the illumination of the Holy Spirit, and the ministries of inspired teaching, admonition, exhortation, and discernment (1 Corinthians 12:4-11; 13:4-8a; 14:1-3).

It will be as if Methodists had been included with the other guests at Martha's home in Bethany, near Jerusalem. "She had a sister named Mary, who sat at the Lord's feet and listened to what he was saying" (Luke 10:39). Like Martha, who was distracted by her many tasks, they will find themselves going to the Lord and comparing themselves with Mary, examining their priorities and realizing that "there is need of only one thing" (Luke 10:41-42). As their priorities come into focus, they will see themselves from the divine perspective and choose to feed upon the Word of the Lord, rather than on the things that satisfy for a little while, but leave the soul malnourished.

Prayer will become a way of enjoying God's presence. Fasting will become a preference for time spent with the Lord. Breaking the fast will become a matter of grace (thanksgiving) at table with the Lord.

The first disciples took bread with Jesus daily. The apostles remembered those meals as sacred time during which Jesus taught with authority. It was this everyday communion with the Lord that allowed them to share his life. In this way, Jesus shaped his followers into women and men who could carry on his work after his death.

Like their fellow Jews, early Christians worshiped in the Temple, synagogue, and at home. The intimate setting of a common room in someone's private apartment, where the extended family, household employees, and neighbors could gather, gave them the privacy and safety in which to break the bread and drink the cup in remembrance of Christ's death. Table fellowship formed the center of community life in the early church

(Acts 2:46-47). Believers repeatedly experienced the presence of the risen Lord with them in the breaking of the bread (Luke 24:30-31).

Just as table fellowship characterized the gatherings of the earliest Christians, coming to the table of the Lord can serve as a metaphor by which contemporary disciples understand the purpose of their meetings. Whether or not literal bread is broken and shared, when the Word of God is read, interpreted, and received, the people of God receive nourishment. They grow until all come into "the unity of the faith and of the knowledge of the Son of God, to maturity, to the measure of the full stature of Christ" (Ephesians 4:13).

Implementing the *Class Meeting* System

Integrating spiritual formation into existing groups cannot be successfully accomplished if it is seen as an "add-on." It must be presented and implemented as a conversion of systems and groups, so that the nurturing ministries of the church support the mission of reaching, making, sustaining, and sending disciples.

1. Study this manual using a highlighter and your Bible. Read the Scripture passages that are cited. Begin using *This Day: A Wesleyan Way of Prayer* on a daily basis. Reflect on your own experience of the spiritual life of your congregation and community, in light of the purpose and goals of the Wesleyan *Class Meeting* and the recommended practice of saying the *daily office.*

2. Learn about the discipleship system that your congregation currently employs. How does your church nurture new Christians and sustain and grow its members toward maturity in Christ? Pray about your role in helping to lead both your church and a class into whole and holy living. Meet with your pastor to share your vision and your understanding of the Wesleyan approach to spiritual formation. Attempt to discern how you should proceed, both in partnership with your pastor and with the policymaking and visioning body of your local church.

3. Meet with the leaders whose responsibility it is to oversee the care of souls and the nurture of adult Christians. Share your vision. Determine the readiness of your congregation to undertake the work of building the congregational infrastructure that John Wesley used so effectively. Involve all those upon whose blessing and cooperation this work will depend

from the beginning. In order to build trust and support, determine how the *Class Meeting* system will be accountable to the leadership structure of the local church. Ask your pastor to become a *Class Leader*.

4. Determine who will coordinate the selection, recruitment, training, and oversight of the *Class Leaders*. The *director* should be fully supportive, trained, and a participant in a *Class Meeting*. Consider asking the pastor to serve as the *director* in charge of the *Class Leaders* in your church.

5. Arrange for a recruitment and training process for all *Class Leaders*, to be guided by your pastor or a lay *director* of discipleship ministries. This manual will serve as the curriculum for the training process. The *Leader's Manual* outlines a ten-hour course of training for *Class Leaders*.

6. Bring *Class Leaders* together as a group of peers for a laboratory experience as a Wesleyan *band* (or *Class Meeting*). Meet weekly for a significant period before deploying participants to organize *Class Meetings*. By using this manual as their study guide, *Class Leaders* will develop skills and experiment with a variety of models for the various elements of the discipleship system, evaluate their experiences, and develop a pattern for *Class Meetings* that they find works well in their local setting. Publicly commission the *Class Leaders*.

7. Having recruited and trained sufficient *Class Leaders* to address the potential in your church, begin interpreting *How Is It With Your Soul?* to the congregation through newsletters, personalized recruitment letters, testimonials during worship, presentations in Sunday school classes, and private conversations. It is essential that everyone who cares to understand receives all available information about dates, time commitment, expectations of class members, how this will affect the existing program of the church, and how the vision of spiritual formation will be implemented as a part of the infrastructure of your church's ministry. Be sure to have your pastor write some of the material that is to be made available. Without the pastor's strong endorsement and active participation, the endeavor will be short-lived and have limited impact.

8. Determine how many classes can be formed, knowing that you need at least three people to form a group. A group of seven people works well. The traditional group size is twelve. The centerpiece of the discipline, the *reflection*, cannot be managed successfully with a group larger than twelve. Note

that a large class that meets in a social hall for education, for example, can be subdivided into smaller groups for the *reflection*. A single class can work in smaller groups of, for example, three, seven, or twelve. In such a case, however, the leaders of those subgroups must be fully trained and must function as consistent *Class Leaders* for a particular group of individuals.

9. Call your class or classes together for an orientation session. You will need between one hour and ninety minutes for the orientation session. The orientation session can be divided into two shorter sessions, if necessary.

Begin with an overview of the plan, emphasizing the biblical and historical bases of the plan, as well as its purpose and components. Outline the three major components of the discipline (daily prayer, regular *Class Meetings*, Scripture study). Distribute *This Day: A Wesleyan Way of Prayer*. Testify to how using the guide to prayer has affected your life.

Say the *daily office* together. Determine what day and time, how frequently, and for how long the class or classes will meet. Choose from among the models provided for the *reflection*, with the understanding that the group will practice strict confidentiality and can revise their plan by consensus at any time.

Give each person a copy of the *General Rules*. Invite the group to suggest contemporary examples of behavior to be avoided and good that members intend to do as a part of their Christian discipleship.

Develop a basic covenant that includes at least the following elements:

We agree:

(1) To use *This Day: A Wesleyan Way of Prayer* on a daily basis, spending between ten and twenty minutes each day in prayer
(2) To meet regularly at a particular time and place
(3) To engage in a specific study or pursue a particular mission as a class
(4) To seek to lead a godly life, following the teaching and example of Jesus

Close with prayer appropriate to your group's culture, followed by a hymn and dismissal with blessing.

10. At the first regular meeting of your class, implement the class session design that you have selected. Distribute copies of the group covenant and review it. Use the *reflection* that your group chose. Follow your plan for at least four weeks before evaluating it formally. Keep a record of your group's comments and progress.

11. Spend a few moments at the close of the fifth class session to review your plan and make any changes that the group feels may be helpful. Measure the appropriateness of these changes against the instruction provided in this manual. Report any changes to the *director*. At any time that significant personal concerns emerge for group members, or a challenge to the discipleship system surfaces within the group, promptly report these concerns to the pastor in charge or to the *director*.

12. Meet monthly with the other *Class Leaders* to hold one another accountable for your discipleship, to share progress and concerns, and to plan for the maintenance and development of your church's discipleship system. Settle in for the long haul. This is a process that will bear fruit over the course of many years. Pray continually. Practice all the means of *grace*.

2

Our Wesleyan Heritage in the Context of the History of Christian Piety

The Roots of the Wesleyan Heritage

The means of *grace*, and the method of practicing them among John Wesley's followers, derive from an ancient tradition. To be short-sighted in our understanding of the history of Christian worship, as if its pure form originated with the Wesley brothers, is to risk ignorance and sectarian elitism, as well as impoverishing the prayer life of the people called Methodists in a new era of seeking after God. When we appreciate the sources and development of Christian practice, we can more intelligently value its most vital elements and discriminate between the essentials of faithfulness and optional or distracting forms of piety.

Wesley made himself a student of Scripture and of the ancient Greek in which the New Testament was written. He also studied the apostolic tradition, the writing of the early church fathers, and the faith and piety of the Protestant Reformers. Moreover, he was an heir to two hundred years of debate and reform in the Church of England. He modeled his method for making disciples of new converts on the prior work of the dissenting churches in Europe and England, as well as the scriptural record of the New Testament churches. His ideal was to restore the life and practice of the primitive church of God. The contemporary *Class Leader's* ability to interpret and encourage use of *This Day: A Wesleyan Guide to Prayer* and the spiritual practices of Methodism will depend, in part, upon an appreciation of the broader context out of which the Wesleyan heritage emerged.

Temple, Synagogue, and Home in First-century Jewish Practice

Jesus, a faithful Jew, grew up attending synagogue. It was there that he learned to worship and first took his place among the people of God. He participated in a simple format for sabbath observance which included recitation of the *Shema* (Deuteronomy 6:4), chanting psalms, reading from the Torah, interpretation of the law by lay teachers, and prayers recited aloud by the congregation. The readings from Scripture followed an annual schedule of readings. The prayers were formal, memorized prayers of praise, confession, thanksgiving, petition, and intercession. At home, Jesus learned to pray several times a day, according to a specific pattern established by Jewish tradition. The vocabulary and phrases of the Lord's Prayer derive from this rich heritage, though the prayer reflects Jesus' particular vision and summarizes the eschatological faith that his followers were to embody.

Not only did Jesus remain a practicing Jew throughout his life, he carried out some of his own teaching ministry in the context of the synagogue (Matthew 4:23; 9:35; Luke 4:16; 13:10). While in Jerusalem, apparently as a part of an annual pilgrimage at the time of Passover, Jesus participated in Temple worship. Temple worship followed the priestly tradition, replete with animal sacrifices and private festival meals.

The Sacrament of Holy Communion emerged out of the Jewish Passover observance held in Jerusalem. The meal would have been eaten amidst the singing of psalms, the retelling of sacred stories, and the recitation of prayers specific to the occasion. The history of God's intervention to save the people was recounted and celebrated, much as it is today among Orthodox Jews at the time of the Passover. Each annual retelling of salvation history brought the people into the divine drama, making them coparticipants with all who lived before them. The festival reinforced the faith that the God of their forefathers remains their God today. Jesus led his disciples to interpret their Jewish faith through his proclamation, "The kingdom of God has come near."

Early Christian Worship Among Jewish Converts

The first Christians were Jews who developed their expectations for worship around prior experiences in the synagogue, temple, and household. They reinterpreted these liturgical patterns in light of Jesus' own practice, his teaching about the nature of God, prayer and fasting, and in light of his death and resurrection. According to Luke and the Acts of the Apostles, they frequently went to the temple to praise God and met in one another's homes to break bread, to pray, and to absorb the apostles' teaching (Luke 24:53; Acts 1:12-14; 2:46-47). The first Christians would have used both the familiar prayers recited in public worship and spontaneous prayers, as did their fellow Jews.

Soon after Jesus' final days in Jerusalem, his disciples began to interpret the life, death, and resurrection of Jesus as the fulfillment of the temple's sacrificial system. At the same time that Jews were rapidly moving away from the sacrificial system, Christians declared Jesus to be the Lamb of God sacrificed for the sins of the world as a ransom for many (1 Corinthians 15:3; Mark 10:45). The same God who gave Israel the sacrificial means of atonement had now provided the ultimate means of salvation in Jesus.

Christians' communal meals were both celebrations of thanksgiving and a means of remembering all that God had done for the world through Jesus. Their sacred meal made them beneficiaries of the life, ministry, death, and resurrection of Jesus. Even more important, they experienced the presence of the risen Lord with them as they broke the bread together in his name.

When persecution forced Christians to flee from Jerusalem into the Gentile world, believers left the practices of the temple behind them and relied on their remembrance of Jesus' teaching and the forms of worship typical of the synagogue. While they worshiped in one another's homes, they also attempted to worship in the local synagogue. When tensions between Jews and Jewish Christians forced Christians to separate themselves from their Jewish neighbors, their gatherings must have looked like a Christian interpretation of synagogue worship.

The *Didache*, an order for the religious life of the Christian community dating from the late first century and early second century, provides early documentation of the developing practices of the Christian church. These and other records suggest that the early church used established liturgical practices, including memorized prayers, singing of the psalms and other hymns, a cycle of readings from the Hebrew Bible, the teachings of the apostles, and a simple meal in remembrance of the Lord's death. These practices provided a setting in which Christians maintained communion with the risen Lord and with one another. Meanwhile, believers continued to engage in private prayer at least three times a day and some maintained other household religious practices based on Jewish patterns. They apparently saw no need to develop a radically new way of honoring God and nurturing their faith. Time was short. All they needed had been provided in their Jewish heritage, whether inherited or adopted, and by their ongoing communion with Christ as Lord.

Early Christian Worship Among Gentiles

As the Gentile missionary churches became the source of normative Christian practice, rather than a mere experiment abroad, Christian worship became increasingly distinct from that of the synagogue. It not only reinterpreted Jewish worship, but also gradually assimilated aspects of Greek and Roman philosophy and religion. The apostle Paul's correspondence indicates the beginnings of this process under his leadership.

Paul was a well-educated Roman citizen nearly as familiar with Greek philosophy and Greco-Roman religion as with Jewish faith and practice. In doing the work of an evangelist, Paul utilized every cultural bridge available to him to communicate with his audience. Among Jews he spoke and behaved as a Jew. Among Greeks, he interpreted his gospel in terms familiar to them.

New converts also brought their prior experiences to Christian worship and influenced the development of a Christian culture. Among the religious expressions that influenced Christian practice were the mystery cults, Gnosticism, Stoicism, neo-Platonism, and the cults built around oracles or ecstatic prophets. Gradually, the teaching and exhortations of presbyters and elders, highly regarded for their faithfulness and knowledge of the apostolic tradition, became authoritative voices that shaped Christian practice and protected it against *syncretism* and heresy.

The letters of Paul and letters attributed to other apostles were preserved, collected, and referred to repeatedly. Some of these writings were canonized as Christian Scripture. They would be used in worship in lieu of the personally delivered teaching of the apostles.

New elements were added to the synagogue-style worship of the early Christians, including inspired preaching and exhortation, Christian hymns and spiritual songs, spontaneous prayers of intercession, thanksgiving, and petition for missionaries and evangelists. Meanwhile, local congregations developed their own unique perspectives, traditions, and practices.

In the fourth century, the Roman Emperor Constantine legalized the practice of Christianity and brought its leaders together into doctrinal councils to formulate creeds and regulate the Christian church. While this process forced dialogue and resulted in a standardization of faith and practice, it also exposed regional differences.

The Establishment of Christianity as the Official Religion of the State

During the late fourth century, an officially funded Christian religious institution housed in temples and basilicas replaced the house churches of the primitive Christian movement. With this transition from worship in relatively small and private settings to gatherings in large public buildings came a shift away from informal worship toward more elaborate liturgy and ritual. This led to a major change in the paradigm for Christian religious practice, both private and public.

The new form of public worship was reminiscent of the imperial activities formerly carried out in these grand public halls. Moreover, Christian worship began to echo the priestly practices of the old Jewish Temple in Jerusalem. Pageantry and responsorial participation by the worshipers, as well as the chanting of the rites, engaged participants and helped make the experience audible to everyone, in the absence of modern sound systems. The Sacrament of Holy Communion became the central event of worship and was reinterpreted as a memorial sacrifice, rather than as a means of communion with the risen Christ.

The church year, replete with observances of the major events of Christ's life and the lives of the martyred saints, replaced the annual pagan festivals that had been scheduled around the lunar calendar. These Christian festivals also replaced the Jewish festivals that early Jewish Christians had observed in commemoration of God's saving acts in the history of the Hebrew people from the beginning of time, such as Passover and Pentecost. The Christian calendar, therefore, became an annual cycle of remembrance and reenactment whereby believers claimed their place in God's redemptive work through Jesus Christ.

By the late fourth century, Christianity was the established religion of the Roman world. It inherited the functions of any major public religion, including providing rites of passage, moral instruction, humanitarian and charitable work, and accountability for civil government to the religious values of the realm. It sought to meet the needs of the masses for festivals, holidays, hero figures, and heroines.

During the waning years of the Roman Empire and throughout the Middle Ages, the distinctive religious practices and styles of worship in the Eastern Orthodox churches and the Roman Catholic tradition were codified. (The liturgies of the Syrian Orthodox and Coptic churches are much older, originating in part from the first century.) Their forms of worship integrate vestiges of the temple cult in Jerusalem, rituals from various indigenous religions, including emperor worship, and the Christian reinterpretation of the imperial realm. Christ reigned over the empire and its populace through the church. With this new and official religion came a priestly and political role for ecclesiastical leaders, a dependent role for laity, and the moral and spiritual corruption that typically accompany wealth and power.

The Monastic Movement

The monastic movement emerged as a reaction to the secularization of the public church. It emphasized private prayer and the pursuit of personal holiness. In the context of this lay separatist movement, the practice of daily hours for prayer resurfaced. Monastic life, governed by a rule of discipline, included praying or singing the psalms and an orderly and extensive reading of Christian Scripture. Monastic piety, practiced in self-contained religious communities, reinterpreted the community life of the early church and emphasized self-denial. A tradition of rigid and meritorious asceticism mirrored early Jewish practice.

The way of life fostered by the monastic movement illustrates a serious attempt to obey Jesus' call to forsake everything to follow him, losing one's life in order to find it. The movement protested the wealth and corruption of the established church. It sought to provide personal salvation for its members and a way of life worthy of Christ, insulated from the temptations of the secular world. Still, it was far removed from the faith and practice of Jesus who mingled daily with the poor, lived among the working class as a Jewish charismatic and a powerful teacher, prophet, healer, and exorcist, and believed that the end of the age was at hand. Its separatism and asceticism limited its usefulness to the masses and had the effect of dividing life between the sacred and secular. It fostered religious elitism even as it challenged the institutionalized church.

The prayer life of the Roman Catholic Church reflects this early history. Its style of worship, liturgy, monastic and other religious orders, priesthood, and theology derive from the role of the church in society from the time of Constantine through the Middle Ages. The Latin Rite, upon which much of Protestant worship would be based, also heavily influenced the practices of the Church of England.

The Renaissance Brought Reform to European Christianity

During the fifteenth- and sixteenth-century Renaissance, faithful men like Zwingli, Luther, and Calvin emerged to challenge the corruption of Christian faith and practice in a new way. Their personal piety and religious culture derived from that of the Roman Catholic Church. They reintroduced the priority of Scripture, transforming not only on its impact on their lives, but on a study of the earliest Christian practices. They attempted to recover New Testament Christianity within their Western European settings, particularly by translating and publishing the

Scriptures in the language of the people. While they reinterpreted the faith through the lens of a fresh reading of Paul's *epistles* and the early church fathers, these reformers preserved the order of worship, the liturgical prayers, and the centrality of the Sacrament of Holy Communion in the new traditions they developed. Empowered by the printing press, Luther and Calvin fostered literacy among the laity by way of the distribution of German and French language Bibles. Their prayer books offered guidance for private and family prayer and thereby restored the central role of the Christian household in the nurture and practice of the faith. The reformers' emphasis on the priesthood of all believers recovered the early Jewish and Jewish Christian practice of lay ministries of the Word, including teaching, exhortation, and other inspired speech.

The reformers encouraged a renewed awareness that all of life is sacred. One no longer needed to live in a religious community to practice the faith and find personal salvation. From the reformers' perspective, salvation and holiness were to be worked out in the practice of one's employment, at home, and in civic responsibility. Discipline was a matter for everyone, though it was to be guided and overseen by pastors who gave themselves to the care of souls through preaching, teaching, visitation, and public liturgy.

The English Reformation

England remained solidly Roman Catholic until Henry VIII rejected papal authority. Even then, the separation between the English church and Rome was more a matter of convenience and economics than of spiritual renewal or theological reform. Through two centuries of bloody civil war, English Puritans and other dissenters fought the powers of the church and the state for religious liberty and the renewal of the Christian faith. Political power shifted repeatedly between those loyal to Rome and the Protestants who preferred worship in the vernacular with a less priestly understanding of Holy Communion. With changes in the British monarchy came changes in the established liturgies of the church, based on the religious sentiments of the reigning monarch. The austerity of Puritan piety and its preference for simplicity of life and worship contrasted dramatically with the pomp and wealth of Rome and the Latin Mass.

Puritans, German Pietists, mystics, and Anabaptists emphasized regeneration, sanctification, and perfection, as well as spontaneous prayer and an inner spiritual life. They regarded the Roman *breviary*, or *daily office* for prayer dating from the ninth century, as a religious form that lacked spiritual power. In the process of the sixteenth-century English Reformation, many religious leaders on both sides gave their lives in the effort to purify the faith. Ultimately, a middle way was forged between the dissenting churches and the established or Roman Catholic Church.

The Church of England

Thomas Cranmer (1489–1556), first Archbishop of Canterbury beginning in 1532, was responsible for shaping the faith and practice of millions, both within and beyond England. He authorized the English Bible, created the English-language liturgy and developed the English breviary or *Book of Common Prayer*. In so doing, he established the pattern for a distinctly Anglican and Protestant Church. The theology of the Church of England and its prayer book relied heavily, however, on the work of the European reformers, particularly Calvin and other Swiss reformers. Its liturgical practices derived from the Gaelic mass as expressed in the liturgy of Salisbury or "Sarum Use," 1085, which gave the church a form for Daily Service, Communion Service, Baptism, and Occasional Offices. (See R. J. Cooke, *History of the Ritual of the Methodist Episcopal Church* [Cincinnati: Jennings and Pye, 1900], pp. 179, 180.) Cranmer opposed the doctrine of transubstantiation, especially the veneration of the elements as the literal body and blood of Christ, and the medieval interpretation of the Eucharist as a sacrificial meal. Largely for these reasons, the archbishop altered the earlier rites to reflect a more Protestant theology of worship and the church. The *Book of Common Prayer* went through several editions, however, and ultimately represented a compromise between those more loyal to the Latin ritual and those who preferred the austere practices of the Puritans.

Wesley's Anglican Roots

It was the 1662 edition of the *Book of Common Prayer* that John Wesley, a priest of the Church of England, used daily. The *daily office*, as well as frequent participation in the Eucharist, usually three times per week, formed Wesley's spiritual practice. The Thirty-nine Articles of Religion, the liturgy for the Lord's Supper, the confessions, and the collects, as well as the system for reading Scripture that the *Book of Common Prayer* made universal for communicants in the Church of England, became normative for British Methodists under John Wesley. This single book and his lifelong use of it, in communion with parish churches, forged in Wesley the belief that only the church can duly provide for the full and proper administration of the means of *grace.*

The Means of *Grace* as John Wesley Practiced Them

Wesley, like his forebears, believed that God gives the divine nature afresh to the people of God through worship, the sacraments, the ministry of the Word, and prayer. This experience of God's saving *grace* transcends rational categories and affirms the active presence of God within history. Wesley and others like him made these claims in bold opposition to enlightenment thought, including scientific rationalism and Deism. The experiential faith of the Methodists filled the void between the liturgy of the Anglican Church and the secular philosophy of the elite. It reached the masses with a life-changing gospel.

The converting gospel that the Wesley brothers and others preached resulted in a spiritual awakening that brought thousands to the faith and placed them in need of further instruction and support. Wesley responded with a methodical approach to spiritual and moral instruction. In so doing, he developed the Methodist *Class Meeting* system and the *General Rules* for the *Class Meetings* as an order for Methodist practice. A prominent feature of the *General Rules* was the practice of the *instituted means of grace*. Among the means of *grace* are the following that Wesley considered essential: searching the Scriptures, prayer, fasting or abstinence, the Lord's Supper, *Christian Conferencing* or conversation, and the public worship of God.

In developing his list of the acts of piety that he expected all Methodists to practice, he drew on the sermons and prayers of Anglican clergy like Jeremy Taylor and William Law. Their devout practice and personal experience of justifying and sanctifying *grace* inspired Wesley's commitment to spreading scriptural holiness throughout the world. It was, therefore, out of Wesley's lifelong faithfulness to the Church of England, as well as his acquaintance with the wider church, both ancient and contemporary, that he developed his understanding of the means of *grace*. From the beginning, therefore, Methodism, like the Church of England, regarded these spiritual practices as keys to conversion and vital to the ongoing pursuit of a right relationship with God.

Searching the Scriptures

Wesley promoted an orderly reading of both the Old and New Testaments, based on the lectionary found in the *Book of Common Prayer*. He rejected the common practice of reading the Bible haphazardly or superstitiously, or reading only one's favorite passages. The Scriptures were to be both read and studied early in the morning and before going to bed at night. In his *Explanatory Notes on the Old Testament*, 1765, Wesley offered careful instruction, in the manner of reading Scripture, including the following: "Read with a single purpose—to know the will of God. Look for the connections between the passage of Scripture being read and the fundamental ideas of Christian faith. Prayerfully seek the guidance and instruction of the Holy Spirit as you read. Resolve to put into practice what God teaches you in your reading and study" (Charles Yrigoyen, Jr., *John Wesley: Holiness of Heart and Life* [Nashville: Abingdon Press, 1996], pp. 41-42). Wesley believed and taught, in concert with the Anglican standard: "We believe the written word of God to be the only and sufficient rule both of Christian faith and practice" *(The Character of a Methodist*, John Wesley, in Welch, p. 293). Thus the Bible was to be read daily by all Methodists and at every opportunity by their leaders. Methodists were to be formed by the Scripture. Moreover, they were to listen for the living Word of God in the context of the entire biblical account of God's saving work, rather than reading in an uninformed and subjective manner.

Prayer

Wesley published many of his own prayers composed for use by children, in the home, and in private. In 1733 he published *A Collection of Forms of Prayer for Every Day of the Week.* It devoted one day of each week to fostering seven virtues by way of Scripture readings, self-examination, and written prayer. Wesley's purpose was to equip his converts for "going on to perfection." He advised:

> Be serious and frequent in the examination of your heart and life. . . . Every evening review your carriage through the day; what you have done or thought that was unbecoming your character; whether your heart has been instant upon religion and indifferent to the world? Have a special care of two portions of time, namely, morning and evening; the morning to fore think what you have to do, and the evening to examine whether you have done what you ought. ("Sermon 105: On Conscience" in vol. 3 *The Works of John Wesley,* ed. Albert Outler [Nashville: Abingdon Press, 1984] p. 488)

By providing formal prayers to be used in the home, Wesley offered every convert the opportunity to live in the world while growing in holiness and being guided by the care and practice of the church. He believed that private prayer that relies either on "inner light," as with the mystics, or on the inclinations of the heart, as with the "enthusiasts," could lead to individualistic religion and heresy. (Wesley parted with William Law over these issues.) The prayers found in the *Book of Common Prayer,* and those derived from the spiritual giants of the past, supplemented by the forms he offered, provided the structure, Wesley believed, for a balanced theology and an adequate spiritual life. He understood the value of spontaneous prayer, however, and encouraged its use two or three days per week (Charles Yrigoyen, Jr., *John Wesley: Holiness of Heart and Life* [Nashville: Abingdon Press, 1996], p. 45). He prayed extemporaneously when ministering to the *band* or class and within the *society* meetings, in response to the diverse needs that he discovered (*Sermon on the Ministerial Office*, 1789 found in Welch, p. 287).

Fasting

Fasting implied prayer. One went without food and beverage in order to focus body, mind, and spirit on God. During most of his life, Wesley followed the ancient pattern of the church in fasting both on Wednesdays and on Fridays. Wednesday was chosen as a way of remembering Judas's betrayal of Jesus. It was to be a day of self-examination, confession, and repentance. Friday was set aside for prayer and meditation on the saving death of Christ. It was to be a solemn day of remembrance and gratitude for divine *grace* revealed through Jesus. He taught that fasting may not be advisable for everyone at all times; however, anyone could benefit by abstaining from certain pleasures, including nonessential food and drink, during concentrated times of prayer. This discipline aided believers in overcoming their physical compulsions and bringing their bodily appetites under the control of the Spirit of God within them (Romans 8:12-13).

Christian Conferencing

Wesley's followers relied on the *connection*, consisting of the class, *band* and *society* meetings, as well as the quarterly and annual conferences of preachers, to preserve and develop their movement. This *connection* ensured that Methodism was an authentic reform movement well equipped to spread and sustain scriptural holiness. The 1884 *Book of Discipline of the Methodist Episcopal Church in America*, for example, listed the *Class Meeting* among the means of *grace* and said that it was essential to the provision of pastoral care for members in light of the itinerancy of pastors. It was, moreover, the key to fostering sound stewardship among the societies and providing financial support for the increasing needs of the movement.

The evangelical experience of regeneration leading to holiness of heart and life, social responsibility, and works of compassion, required ongoing discipline through the *Class Meeting* system. It also required continuous theological *reflection* throughout the *connection*. *Christian Conferencing*, or spiritual and theological conversation, provided a means of sustaining and reforming faithfulness. The beliefs and practices that would become the hallmarks of Methodism, such as the *General Rules* (1743) and the revised Articles of

Religion contained in the Sunday Service for the American Church, were first worked out in connectional settings for *Christian Conferencing*.

Liturgical Practice: The Lord's Supper and the Public Worship of God

All Methodists were to worship at their parish church on the Lord's Day. The historic liturgy of the church linked Methodists with the wider church and the communion of the saints. Above all, the public proclamation of the Word and the celebration of the sacraments kept believers within the authority and *grace* of God's saving purpose. The Lord's Supper was to be received whenever it was offered as the supreme means of partaking of the preventing, justifying, and sanctifying *grace* of God through Christ. No sincere person was excluded from the Lord's Table. Nothing was required for participation other than repentance and faith in Christ. Wesley believed that a communicant could actually be converted—that is, led to faith and repentance, by partaking of the Sacrament.

Occasional Services

In addition to Sunday worship and *society* meetings, however, Wesley led a revival of occasional services of worship. Foremost among them were the Love Feast and the annual *Covenant Service*. The Love Feast, first introduced to Wesley by the German Moravians, was modeled on the communal meals of the early church during which the believers testified to experiencing the presence of the risen Lord in their midst. He advocated using it quarterly with the *bands* of women's and men's classes, for the purpose of mutual encouragement and celebration in Christian community. He wrote: "At these love feasts ... our food is only a little plain cake and water. But we seldom return from them without being fed, not only with the 'meat which perisheth,' but with 'that which endureth to everlasting life'" (Welch, p. 185). Today the service includes light refreshments of bread and water. This central feature—a simple meal that symbolizes feeding on the bread of life, Jesus the Christ, and treasuring the spring of water welling up within the believer, the Spirit given to the church—allows lay ministers to preside (John 4:13-14; 6:35; 7:38-39).

The Love Feast is not a Sacrament like the Lord's Supper. It recalls key images of the gospel and provides for deepening Christian fellowship through spontaneous prayer, an abundance of singing, and testimonies to the *grace* of God. Participants set their witness of faith in the context of a biblical passage that they read aloud. The service often leads to something

Methodists call a melting of the heart or "hearts strangely warmed" (see also Luke 24:32).

The *Covenant Service* was adopted in 1765 as a "means of increasing serious religion" (Charles Yrigoyen, Jr., *John Wesley: Holiness of Heart and Life*, p. 53). Methodists still use an abbreviated form of it on New Year's Eve or on the Sunday nearest the New Year. The liturgy provides a worshipful setting for corporate self-examination, confession, repentance, forgiveness of sins, and renewal of total devotion to Christ. Wesley urged that the covenant be signed and dated by each Methodist, to be reviewed the following year. The occasional services, coupled with regular observance of the Sunday service and the *Class Meeting* system, preserved the regenerative experience of conversion and provided for lifelong Christian discipleship, as well as the assurance of salvation beyond physical death.

Wesley's Pattern and the Growing Methodist Movement

Wesley expected all Methodists to derive their belief system and way of life from the standard practice of the Church of England. He remained a loyal member of the Church of England to his death. In developing a pattern of Sunday service to be used by Methodists in America, including an order for morning and evening prayer, Wesley abbreviated the *Book of Common Prayer* and amended it slightly. Although he recommended the elimination of most of the thirty-nine holy days observed by the Anglican tradition, he advised Methodists to observe Christmas Day, Good Friday, Easter Day, Ascension Day, Whitsunday (Pentecost), and Trinity Sunday (James F. White, *A Brief History of Christian Worship* [Nashville: Abingdon Press, 1993], p. 162). Wesley emphasized the importance of a weekly celebration of the Eucharist.

Methodist Prayer and Liturgical Practice Since Wesley

In his *History of the Methodists*, Jesse Lee, an eighteenth-century Methodist historian, wrote:

> For some time the preachers generally read prayers on the Lord's-day, and in some cases the preachers read part of the morning service on Wednesdays and Fridays; but some who had been accustomed to pray extempore were unwilling to adopt this new plan, being fully satisfied that they could pray better and with more devotion while their eyes were shut than they could with their eyes open. After a few years, the

Prayer-book was laid aside, and has never been used since in public worship. (p. 170)

American Methodists used the liturgy for Holy Communion as prescribed by Wesley in his publication *The Sunday Service of the Methodists in North America* (London, 1784) but otherwise preferred a simpler approach to corporate and private worship. The early preachers led the people in extemporaneous prayer and "took a text" from which to preach. The order of worship usually included singing, prayer, the reading of Scripture, and preaching, followed by "opening the doors of the church" (an invitation to Christian discipleship through conversion and membership), closing prayer, and the apostolic benediction from 2 Corinthians 13:13. The 1884 *Book of Discipline of the Methodist Episcopal Church* included an order for congregational morning and evening prayer, modeled after that of the *Book of Common Prayer*. One can assume that while few laity owned this book, all lay preachers and clergy not only owned a copy but respected its instruction.

British Methodists did not publish a prayer book for general use until the twentieth century. When it was introduced, the conservative Methodists in the north of England rejected it, due to its obvious kinship with the Anglican *Book of Common Prayer*. From their point of view, the middle way of the Anglican Church was a compromise with popery that many British Methodists found untenable.

British and North American Methodists of the late eighteenth and nineteenth centuries knew no standard lectionary or other pattern of prescribed lessons. Lay preachers often provided for the ministry of the Word, proclaiming the gospel with great emotional intensity and spiritual power, but without the benefit of formal training. While ordained clergy preached from a biblical text, exhorters did not.

The Methodists learned their theology through singing hymns, rather than by way of instruction or liturgy. Formal prayers seemed alien in the back woods, on the farm, on the frontier, or among the working class of the industrial cities. The itinerancy of ordained clergy led to infrequent celebration of the Sacraments of Holy Communion and baptism; thus, only occasional use was made of the authorized and somewhat lengthy form for the Eucharist, with its Service of Morning Prayer, originally designed to precede Holy Communion.

With prosperity and the settled pastorate, however, came education, more elaborate houses of worship, and standardized worship patterns. By the late nineteenth century, the Course of Study in the Methodist Episcopal Church required candidates for ordained ministry to study rhetoric and sermon preparation. A more elaborate order of worship was published in the official hymnals of the twentieth century. More Scripture was read in the Sunday Service, and formal prayer became a regular feature of congregational worship.

The 1940 *Book of Discipline of the Methodist Church*, for example, included an order for morning and evening prayer to be used by individuals and groups. By 1967, *The Book of Worship* offered a pattern for daily morning and evening prayer to be used in the home. A similar resource was included in the *United Methodist Book of Worship*, 1989, for use with small groups, with no mention of its use by either the individual or the family. The revival of a standard form for daily prayer among Methodists, equivalent to the "Sarum Use" of A.D. 1085, and similar to the ritual treasured by the Wesley brothers, would wait for the twenty-first century.

The *General Rules* and the *Class Meeting*

The *General Rules* were to be kept by all Methodists as a means of discipline. In outline form, they were: avoid evil of every kind, do all the good you can, practice the means of *grace*. *Class Meetings* were to be governed by these rules as by a mutual covenant with God.

This English Protestant equivalent of the monastic rule addressed the cry of Antinomianism or lawlessness hurled at evangelicals in light of their doctrine of salvation by *grace* through faith alone. Nonetheless, Wesley wrote:

> We do not place the whole of religion (as too many do, God knoweth) either in doing no harm, or in doing good, or in using the ordinances of God. No not in all of them together; wherein we know that a man may labour many years, and at the end have no religion at all, no more than he had at the beginning. (*The Character of a Methodist* in Welch, p. 295)

Methodists relied entirely on the *grace* of God revealed in Jesus Christ for their salvation. No work of piety, penance, or service could contribute anything to personal salvation. At the same time, they considered faith without holiness of heart and life empty and fruitless. According to Wesley's doctrine, the regenerative power of the gospel leads through justifying *grace* to sanctifying *grace*, whereby the believer becomes obedient to the faith and teachings of Jesus. Any Methodist worthy of admission to the *society* meetings was expected to continue to demonstrate the desire "to flee from the wrath to come" by adhering to the *General Rules* and participating faithfully in its weekly *Class Meetings*.

These gatherings encouraged believers to "watch over one another in love" (1 John 4:7) and to bear witness to their faith. Through *Christian Conferencing* and conversation, the Methodist experience of saving *grace* was sung, proclaimed, and clarified for the benefit of both the new converts and the most seasoned leaders. To this day, the *Class Meeting* provides the setting in which believers are encouraged and uphold one another in ongoing discipleship. In addition, the *Class Meeting* enables responsible study of Scripture and theological *reflection* by the laity.

The Social Principles and the *General Rules*

The *instituted means of grace*, as Wesley understood and promoted them, derive from the practices of Jesus and the early church. They may be considered acts of devotion, since they enable believers to express their love for God and promote personal holiness. Wesley believed that faithfulness also includes personal moral discipline and "works of mercy," in the context of a supportive community. Good judgment required that Methodists meet to encourage one another to avoid evil of every kind and do good at every opportunity. He called this practice a *prudential means of grace.*

The discipline that Methodists practiced emerged out of a larger vision of God at work for the redemption of every aspect of private and public life. Methodism addressed both individual practice and the priorities and practices of the society at large. The Wesley brothers taught, demonstrated, and sang the prophetic message that God's saving work includes establishing justice and caring for the most vulnerable, as well as saving souls.

Wesley lived simply, saving all he could from his publishing efforts in order to be able to give generously to the poor. He established infirmaries, schools, and homes for widows and orphans. He influenced political leaders by his opposition to slavery and his effort to enhance public health. His work in the prisons, especially among debtors, inspired lay initiatives toward prison reform. He worked to reform alcoholics and led his movement in abstinence from "spirituous liquors," which negatively affected family life. This emphasis contributed to lifting many households out of poverty and violence.

The spiritual descendants of John and Charles Wesley have continued their work. Methodism seeks to apply the mandate to love God and neighbor in practical ways, thereby cooperating with the redeeming *grace* of God in every dimension of life. The World Methodist Social Affirmation, frequently used in public worship as a statement of faith, interprets the early Methodist vision in contemporary terms (*The United Methodist Hymnal* [Nashville: United Methodist Publishing House, 1989], #886).

Twenty-first-century Methodists must struggle with an ever-changing moral and political climate. They must discern for themselves which of the values and practices that are common in their setting clearly under-mine the well-being of humanity and the natural world, in order to agree not only to avoid them but to address them constructively. This theologi-cal work requires reference to the Scriptures, especially the example and teaching of Jesus, the record of the church's thought and practice, all available scientific insight, and the highest powers of reasoning and spir-itual wisdom. It also requires experimentation, courageous risk-taking, and diligent advocacy.

The Methodist *Class Meeting* provides a forum for Christian conversa-tion around complex ethical concerns. For this reason, both the work of supporting one another's personal practice of faithfulness and the cur-riculum chosen for study need to be deliberately directed toward address-ing the full spectrum of moral, political, economic, familial, and social concerns. An adequate practice of Methodism and leadership of the *Class Meeting* can only be achieved by way of a comprehensive perspective on holiness of heart and life.

3

Nurturing Discipleship Through the Twenty-first Century Wesleyan *Class Meeting* System

The People of God in Mission

Since the decline of the *Class Meeting* system in the United States during the late nineteenth century and the institutionalization of what was the Methodist movement, the mission of the church has increasingly focused on maintaining its membership and preserving the role of the church in the larger society. During the late nineteenth and early twentieth centuries, Methodists fostered the spread of Western civilization around the world through foreign mission work, but they did little to convert either themselves or the majority populations in their own neighborhoods to the vision and practice of Christian discipleship. The weakening of moral and spiritual discipline among the laity, coupled with increasing dependency upon professional clergy for leadership, resulted in a precipitous decline in the church's impact on the lives of its members and on the society at large.

Moving Beyond Membership to Discipleship

It is time now to call the people of God beyond membership to mission, beyond cultural Christianity to dynamic faith and witness, and beyond passive voluntarism into ministry in the Spirit and integrity of Jesus. Vital to this transition is a recovery of Jesus' own rule for discipleship: "If any want to become my followers, let them deny themselves and take up their cross and follow me. For those who want to save their life will lose it, and those who lose their life for my sake, and for the sake of the gospel, will save it" (Mark 8:34-35). Note that Jesus addressed the crowds along with his disciples, as if to distinguish between those who are seeking something for themselves and those who want to serve as Jesus' representatives in the world.

The life of discipleship is costly. It involves sacrifice and resistance. It also brings the highest possible fulfillment and joy. Members of Methodist *Class Meetings* in the twenty-first century will be among those who make the difficult choice to respond to the call to belong to Jesus on Jesus' terms. They will identify with the apostle Paul when he wrote: "Paul, a servant of Jesus Christ, called to be an apostle, set apart for the gospel of God ... to bring about the obedience of faith among all the Gentiles for the sake of his name, including yourselves who are called to belong to Jesus Christ" (Romans 1:1, 5-6).

A Contemporary Discipleship System

Every effective faith community engages in reaching out to meet people where they are, relating them to God, nurturing them in the faith, caring for them as whole persons over the course of their participation, and then training and deploying them to reach out in effective ministry beyond the boundaries of the faith community. Over the course of time, relationships form that become increasingly meaningful expressions of divine love. It is out of these relationships that some of the most durable and transformational Christian experiences occur. Rarely does a conversion that takes place in a major evangelistic rally or through a personal crisis result in lifelong discipleship without the immediate association of that fresh faith experience with a faith community. Believers must be nurtured by others like themselves who accept the responsibility to care and to be cared for. The *Class Meeting* provides a structure within which nurturing can take place.

For these reasons, *Class Leaders* can be instrumental in seeing people through the life cycle of faith and helping them to remain faithful. They can provide the authentic care necessary to help guests become disciples and new members become lay ministers. *Class Leaders* can be the single most effective people in ministering healing in the midst of disenchantment or alienation and in caring for people who are going through crisis. Moreover, the traditional role of the *Class Leader* is to foster ongoing financial stewardship among the members. For these reasons, the *Class Leader* functions as a lay pastor to the members of his or her class and as an essential member of the ministry team in the local church. When the leadership of a local church understands the ministry of nurturing disciples through the Wesleyan *Class Meeting* system, it will make the development and maintenance of the *Class Meeting* system its priority.

Exploring the Need for a Discipleship System: Developing a Shared Vision

The almost invisible and insignificant beginnings of your dream of helping people in your area become mature in faith can become a ministry that redeems the lives of real people and transforms the life of your congregation. Jesus suggested that the kingdom of God is like yeast hidden in a huge quantity of dough, like a seed that must be sown in order to bring forth a harvest, like a pearl of great price, or like a field with a treasure in it. The kingdom of God is so valuable that possessing it is worth surrendering everything else in which one is invested. The vision has tremendous potential for producing the highest form of good. It will be realized out of a faith response to Jesus, careful and prayerful study of his teaching, the need of the church to form disciples, and a tenacious devotion to the work of God on the part of a few faithful leaders in your community. Nevertheless, the work of spiritual formation often seems slow, relatively fruitless, and fraught with difficulties. To succeed as a *Class Leader*, you must have a clear and compelling vision.

The groundwork for developing a shared vision for ministries that form disciples of Christ among the laity must be done over time. A series of courses, sermons, conversations, a needs assessment process, and a retreat can provide for the necessary processing and consensus building within a congregation. Among the topics and resources relevant to the process include:

- A study of Craig Miller's book *NextChurch.now* (Nashville: Discipleship Resources, 1999)

- A study of the early Methodist *Class Meeting* and of John Wesley's application of the *General Rules* in Charles Yrigoyen, Jr., *John Wesley: Holiness of Heart and Life* (Nashville: Abingdon Press, 1996)

- A study of faith development over the course of the life span within small groups in Thomas R. Hawkins, *Cultivating Christian Community* (Nashville: Discipleship Resources, 2001)

- Small group leadership in Thomas R. Hawkins, *The Christian Small-Group Leader* (Nashville: Discipleship Resources, 1989)

- Marjorie Thompson's book *Soul Feast: An Invitation to the Christian Spiritual Life* (Louisville: Westminster John Knox Press, 1995)

- Steven W. Manskar, *Accountable Discipleship: Living in God's Household* (Nashville: Discipleship Resources, 2001)

- David Lowes Watson, *The Early Methodist Class Meeting: Its Origins and Significance* (Nashville: Discipleship Resources, 1985)

- Steven W. Manskar, *A Perfect Love: Understanding John Wesley's 'Plain Account of Christian Perfection'* (Nashville: Discipleship Resources, 2003)

- Henry Knight, *Eight Life-Enriching Practices of United Methodists* (Nashville: Abingdon Press, 2001)

- Ted Campbell, *Methodist Doctrine: The Essentials* (Nashville: Abingdon Press, 1999)

These resources can be circulated among the leaders of your church. Pastors and lay officers can use regular meetings of the church for brief teaching moments based on these resources.

Assessing Your Congregation's Need for Discipleship Ministries

Study your church's vital signs over the past decade. Include a survey of membership records regarding numbers of persons received on confession of faith and your church's retention of new members. Investigate how many needs-based ministries were initiated. Determine how many new lay leaders were identified, recruited, trained, deployed, and effective in ministry. Analyze these data as they inform your sense of the effectiveness of the congregation's ministry of making disciples.

Determine how participation in faith-based study, action, spiritual formation, and support groups was developed. What worked best and why? What didn't work and why not? Investigate patterns of conflict and conflict resolution. Most of this information can be gleaned from newsletters, statistical reports, and minutes of annual meetings.

A thorough needs assessment, however, should not be limited to statistical analysis. A thorough assessment includes interviews with members regarding their experience with the means of *grace*. These interviews, especially when they represent a diverse sampling of the congregation, will encourage reflection and conversation among those not in leadership positions. It will also provide insight into member concerns that leaders should take to their visioning process.

Usually, the conclusion of such a survey will point to the need for deepening discipleship within the local church, in order to empower the laity to fulfill their ministries and move beyond dependency, maintenance, stagnation, survival, or conflict. Patiently prepared groundwork, done over the course of several months through a thorough needs assessment, will provide a sense of mandate and foster broad ownership of the discipleship system that emerges from it.

Why Meet as a Class?

In the past, many *Class Leaders* have compromised the practice both of Jesus and of John Wesley by attempting to care for their members solely on an individual basis. They do this because the members resist participating in a covenanted group that meets regularly and because the work of recruiting and maintaining a class can seem greater than caring for people individually. Some suggest that one-on-one care overcomes concerns about privacy, fosters greater intimacy, and is more readily received. The disadvantages of such an approach, however, tempting as it is, outweigh the advantages.

Caring for individuals separately is time consuming. It often must be done while other family members are present. For those who live alone or find it difficult to participate in *Class Meetings*, home visits may create dependency rather than empower accountable discipleship.

Too often in the context of private visits, conversation between *Class Leader* and member devolves into a merely social contact. Prayer tacked on at the end of the visit is usually focused on the felt needs of the member. The *Class Leader* feels fulfilled and needed. The member feels cared for. Usually, however, neither has effectively called the other into transformational discipleship.

Visitation of the homebound represents a necessary compromise in the usually recommended approach to caring for members. This exception to the rule poses a special challenge to engage the shut-in or ill person in meaningful discipleship, rooted in an active sense of participation in the faith community. Every effort should be made to take the class to the shut-in or to transport the shut-in to the class, unless a disability absolutely precludes group participation.

While the challenges of caring for people in a small group setting are many and ongoing, the Wesleyan *Class Meeting* system has proved itself both efficient and vastly more productive over the long-term than individual visitation or counseling. Visiting from house to house or by way of casual contact, including telephone calls may, however, provide a necessary starting place for people who resist a greater commitment. It can be an interim means of maintaining contact through times of transition. It is vital for you to be clear that the sincere seeker will need to become and to remain a part of the faith community in order to enjoy the fullness of the Christian experience.

The many benefits of bringing people together for mutual support and instruction in discipleship become visible over time. Among them are the following:

1. Overcoming isolation
2. Deepening spiritual fellowship
3. Exchanging supportive and constructive criticism for growth in discipleship
4. Feedback, prayer, and friendship through spiritually desolate times and through personal crises
5. Education and training for ministry, enriched by group dynamics and the presence of the risen Christ where two or more are gathered in his name
6. Partnership for ministries to be carried on in reaching out to the world through acts of witness, mercy, and justice

Recruiting Class Members

As a *Class Leader* you will need to begin recruiting your class members by way of personal contact. Through these personal contacts, meaningful relationships of mutual trust and shared understanding develop. These initiatives will serve as the first steps toward effective Christian caregiving.

Do not rely primarily on announcements in the church newsletter, bulletin, or from the pulpit to gather your class. Rarely is it advisable to divide your congregation geographically and assign neighborhoods to a *Class Leader*. Instead, personally invite people who may genuinely desire to grow in faith to join your class.

Meet with other *Class Leaders* to agree on who will approach whom. Work hard over the course of three to four weeks to gather twelve members. Report the names of the people you have contacted and the names of those who have agreed to participate in your class to the *director* on a weekly basis. This will ensure that other *Class Leaders* avoid contacting the same people. The *director* will keep a careful record of recruitment efforts and communicate with all *Class Leaders* at least once a week. This method will provide a gauge of progress and contribute to a sense of developing momentum. Post class rosters, including the time and place of meetings, on a prominent bulletin board in the church building. If you begin with seven people, get started within four weeks of the first contact, well before the interest and commitment level of those who have agreed to participate wanes. Then encourage the original members to invite others to join.

Alternative Groupings for Accountable Discipleship

Class Meetings can have several functions. The standard format for the Wesleyan *Class Meeting* includes three elements: (1) prayer, (2) mutual accountability around a shared covenant, and (3) study. Other formats and settings can foster accountable discipleship as well. When the local church respects the time and energy limitations of its members, it often finds that existing small groups within its ministry structure should be transformed into *Class Meetings* in order to ensure that all members are actively engaged in a discipleship system while contributing to the mission of the church.

Employing the *Class Meeting* System Within Ministry Teams

Ministry teams, as well as adult educational classes, benefit from employing the covenantal practices and group *reflection* of the Wesleyan *Class Meeting*. The ministry team or other committee uses all of the elements of the Wesleyan *Class Meeting* system, except the curriculum for adult education. It replaces the usual study component with its own ministry function.

When we lay ministers gather to accomplish a task, we arrive from as many circumstances and with as many different agendas as there are individuals in the group. Our tendency is to focus on getting the job done on the basis of skills and patterns familiar to us from our secular employment and civic groups. By intentionally gathering in the presence of Christ, the ministry team sets the stage for exercising ministry in the name and in the Spirit of Jesus. By opening ourselves to one another, we examine ourselves and check in with our peers. When team members describe the state of our souls and share either triumph or struggle, our fellowship deepens. Our group becomes one body in tune with itself. Potential team dysfunction can be addressed before it derails the mission of the group. In the *Class Meeting*, we receive the personal support we need and deserve. We feel heard, valued, and understood. We get what we need and can give more generously as a result.

Some churches use a slightly different model in which all small groups engage in four activities: (1) mutual care, (2) personal spiritual life, (3) study, and (4) mission. The group is free to determine what its primary mission or service component will be and how much emphasis it will place on the four components of group life. Each group develops its own culture for fulfilling the various aspects of group life, while taking care to watch over one another in love in light of the *General Rules*. In this case, everyone would be encouraged to use *This Day: A Wesleyan Way of Prayer*, live a godly life as described by the *General Rules*, and engage in the work of ministry through their unit of the church.

When existing groups are converted into *Class Meetings*, the leaders and members must be invited into the process of visioning, training, experimentation, covenanting, and regular evaluation of the Wesleyan discipleship system as early as possible. Some existing groups and group leaders will resist, making the *Class Meeting* system untenable for their group. Members of a long established choir, for example, may find that altering the patterns of that ministry team will be difficult. These members will need and want to participate in an adult Sunday school class that is committed to being a Wesleyan *Class Meeting*. The ideal is that all active members of your church will understand their participation in the faith community to include membership in a *Class Meeting* or ministry team that engages in the Wesleyan discipleship system.

Creating Sacred Space for the *Class Meeting*

The setting for your group's meeting should be conducive to quiet *reflection* and prayer, as well as confidential conversation. Schedule and prepare the space in advance. When determining which space to use and what equipment may be required, consider the particular needs of your group for lighting, acoustics, seating, temperature control, work space, markerboard, overhead projector, printed resources, visual aids, and a worship center. Keep in mind that your purpose is to create sacred space where your participants can feel comfortable, safe, and supported.

Be intentional about your seating arrangement. Groups usually function best when members can see one another's faces. This facilitates active listening on everyone's part and allows the leader to function as an active participant.

Many classes and other faith-based small groups use a visual focal point to draw attention to the presence of God in their midst and to remind them of their primary mission. Ideally, the images you choose will emerge out of your group's vision and covenant. Until the class identifies a particular image as one that speaks to and for them, you can inspire a sense of the presence of God throughout the session by introducing a variety of visual metaphors.

Set a small table in the center of the gathering space or dedicate the center of your conference table to the focal point you wish to create. The table may be draped and set with a still life that invites your members into worship. Examples of appropriate symbols include a cross, a cross and flame, a lighted candle with an open Bible, a basin of water and a towel, a loaf of bread and a pitcher of water, a decanter of water and clear cups, an image of praying hands or outstretched hands. The visual aid can serve both to refocus your group when it strays from its mission and as a focal point for meditation. By integrating colors, textures, symbols, and the arts, you encourage more full participation by visual learners and quiet, reflective personalities.

The Group Covenant: Creating and Maintaining a Group Culture

Group consensus on what is expected of your class members supports a healthy, sustainable class. John Wesley's *General Rules* provide a historic reference and starting place for a contemporary rule of order for Methodist *Class Meetings*. Earlier resources include the Sermon on the Mount (Matthew 5–7:27), Acts 2:44-47, and the *Didache* (a rule for Christian community dating from the late first century and early second century A.D.). Study and interpret these in light of their original purpose, to aid followers of Jesus to remain alert and prepared for ministry in Jesus' name. These guides must not be used as a new form of legalism or a way of determining who is welcome and who is excluded. With the biblical and historic background firmly in place, your class can determine what its priorities will be and how members will seek to achieve and maintain the discipline of holy living.

Determine to uphold the standard that Jesus himself provided: "If any want to become my followers, let them deny themselves and take up their cross and follow me. For those who want to save their life will lose it, and those who lose their life for my sake, and for the sake of the gospel, will save it" (Mark 8:34-35). Three elements must be included, therefore, in any adequate rule of discipleship: (1) a continuing desire to follow Jesus, (2) self-denial, including accepting rejection and persecution for the sake of the gospel, (3) and willingness to go and do what the demands of the gospel require. Authentic disciples of Christ observe Jesus' rule diligently and prefer the work of living and spreading the news of God's reign to other values and purposes, no matter how worthy or desirable they may be.

Jesus' rule is difficult to follow; however, it remains a saving rule. Apart from understanding, accepting, and practicing this rule, would-be Christians either lose their way or never get started. All the practices and beliefs of the Christian religion, without the clarity of purpose and discipline of Jesus' rule, will only lead to losing one's soul and one's relationship with God. There is no substitute for the life wholly consecrated to the gospel. The question that remains is: *How shall this life of faithfulness to God be practiced within the lives of the twenty-first century Methodists who agree to form a new class?*

Some might advise that *Class Leaders* introduce the moral and spiritual practices of Methodism gradually, with the intention of leading members toward an increasingly holistic and consistent discipline over time. The impediment in this approach is that once the culture of your group is established, both you and your members tend to relax the standard rather than strengthen it. For this reason, we recommend that the discipline required by Jesus serve as the standard for Methodist classes from their inception and that the *General Rules* be upheld as their historic application. The contemporary expression of discipleship should be written as a covenant with God through the faith of Jesus, in the form of a community rule. When formulated within these parameters, it will be worthy of true disciples of Jesus and will be clearly focused on supporting lifelong holiness of heart and life.

Sample Covenant for a Methodist Class Meeting

The covenant given below is an example that may be used to develop a covenant for the Class Meeting.

As a class of Methodists who earnestly desire to follow Jesus in (your city/town, and state), we solemnly agree, to the best of our ability and by the power of God's Word and Spirit:

1. To avoid every form of evil, including all practices that undermine either the well-being of ourselves or of others
2. To accept the social, emotional, economic, and other costs involved in moral and spiritual faithfulness to the teachings of Christ
3. To pursue the work of ministry together through acts of witness, mercy, and justice

We will support one another in so doing by:

- Meeting together on a regular basis
- Searching the Scriptures both together and at home

- Joining the congregation for weekly worship
- Partaking of the Lord's Supper whenever it is offered
- Praying daily, using *This Day: A Wesleyan Way of Prayer* as a guide
- Abstaining from specific practices that tend toward self-indulgence, spiritual and moral distraction, or interfere either with our relationship with God or with fulfilling our mission and ministry and
- Fasting at agreed upon times of concentrated prayer

Signed and dated by all members

Class Norms

An addendum to the class covenant, subject to quarterly or annual review, should address the following considerations:

1. Frequency, timing, and length of meetings
2. Any alternative daily spiritual practices that may be shared by all members
3. Group confidentiality
4. The method to be used within the class sessions for the *reflection*
5. Who will lead, and the term and conditions of office for the leader
6. How the group will care for those who fail to keep the covenant or show signs of discontent, personal crisis, or other special needs
7. How the class session will be organized and what the content will be
8. When and how new members will be received into the class and current members will be released from the covenant
9. When the covenant will be evaluated and renewed

One local church's statement regarding norms for its *Class Meetings* illustrates the way a particular class agreed to function:

> We will practice confidentiality regarding any personal matters that are shared by class members, encourage others to join our class after interpreting the covenant to them, and support one another in the life of discipleship through any times of personal struggle or special need. Our Class Meetings will begin with a prayer for illumination followed by a time of sharing, during which the Class Leader will inquire, "How is it with your soul?" We will come to class prepared to report on our progress or struggles in keeping the covenant and growing in our faithfulness to God and one another. This portion of our Class Meeting will

take between ten and fifteen minutes. We will begin our formal study within fifteen minutes of the stated hour for our class session. The study time will be based on questions or topics that members bring to the attention of the class after having studied the biblical references in the textbook as well as the textbook at home. We will attempt to cover one chapter each week. We will close our class sessions with prayer for one another, taking care to name any concerns that have emerged during class time, followed by the Lord's Prayer. We will evaluate our covenant during our sixth session and recovenant at that time for ongoing ministry and discipleship.

Maintaining the *Class Meeting* System

Take care to protect against perceptions on the part of nonparticipants that classes are producing a form of elitism within the congregation. To ensure the durability and the continuing effectiveness of the *Class Meetings*, communicate with the congregation, evaluate progress, and intentionally incorporate new people. Communicate at least quarterly with the leadership of the church regarding the development and impact of the discipleship system, including any changes in *Class Leaders*. Be sure that retiring and new *Class Leaders* are officially recognized. Communicate with class members, particularly those who may be absent for more than one *Class Meeting* or who miss more than two consecutive Sunday worship services. Report news of the classes to the congregation through all available means, including an occasional testimonial in worship by a member who can personally attest to the value of the method being used for spiritual formation. Develop and implement a plan for ongoing leadership recruitment, supervision, and training. Determine a strategy for forming new groups and for filling vacancies in existing classes. Preserve an atmosphere of hospitality and a culture of inviting discipleship, while maintaining the covenant and the vision of maturing in Christ.

Establish an anniversary weekend or a quarterly renewal weekend as a time of celebration. Include a Wesleyan Love Feast with singing, prayer, testimonials, and a brief exhortation on the theme of discipleship. Renegotiate or reaffirm the class covenant. Introduce new members to the *Class Meeting* system at this time and include them in an actual class session.

The Love Feast, quarterly meeting, or other renewal format can serve as a helpful break in the pattern of the *Class Meeting* if it takes place during the time when your groups usually meet. It can also serve as a means of transition into new study material. Be wary, however, of interrupting the flow of the weekly class schedules. Once a healthy pattern has been established, don't risk breaking it.

Forming New Groups and Integrating Newcomers

As a general rule, one new class should be formed for every eight newcomers to a congregation. The method you choose for integrating newcomers will work best, however, when it takes into account the particular characteristics of your church. For example, a large and growing church with many *Class Meetings* will function best by creating a new class for newcomers at least once each quarter. A midsize church, growing at a moderate rate, may need to introduce newcomers to existing *Class Meetings* once a quarter. A small church that is growing one family unit at a time and has only one or two existing *Class Meetings* may be successful in integrating newcomers upon receiving them into membership in the church. In any case, the process of hospitality must gracefully welcome the stranger as one of God's people called to holiness of heart and life (Romans 1:7a).

New Member Training: Introducing the Discipleship System Early

The new member training process within any local church can include the formation of a new *Class Meeting*. Within this initial membership orientation process, newcomers learn about the mission of the church and its discipleship system. They gain a sense of the history of the Methodist movement and of their place in its ongoing story. Newcomers feel less intimidated when meeting with others like themselves who are just beginning to belong to the faith community. By initiating new members into the vision and culture of discipleship in this way, you allow them to be formed by the highest ideals of your discipleship system from the beginning.

When forming a new class as the springboard for new member training seems difficult to achieve, as it does in many settings, alternatives can work as well. If you find, for example, that your new members have conflicting schedules or seem to have very little in common, it may be more profitable to help them find existing groups that will meet their needs. First take the time to meet with them privately to explore their interests, needs, and readiness. Then notify the *Class Leader* to whom you will refer the newcomer, being careful to limit the size of each class to twelve. Introduce the newcomer to the *Class Leader* in advance. The *director* of the *Class Meeting* system and the person in charge of new member integration will want to work together to support the newcomer and the *Class Leader* in their new relationship.

Essential components of the process of integrating a newcomer into an existing group include friendly introductions and an orientation to the norms and covenant of the specific class. When a class meets and greets a newcomer, as *Class Leader* you will need to take more time than usual to gather the group and foster a sense of hospitality. For this reason, many classes create a fellowship time before the session begins, when you can informally introduce the newcomer to several members of the group with whom the newcomer may identify.

An alternative is to welcome newcomers quarterly, on the occasion of the Love Feast and renewal weekend. This allows the newcomer to enter at a natural point of transition in the life of the class. When this pattern is followed, newcomers do not feel they are breaking into a closed group.

Leadership: Who Should Lead?

As a *Class Leader*, you should be a member in good standing who exemplifies active discipleship and has already demonstrated the ability to lead, to listen, to care for others, to maintain confidentiality, and to speak concisely and clearly. You should have completed sufficient biblical and theological training to guide others within a biblical framework of Christian faith and practice. You should have a working knowledge of the Church, its teaching, and its practice. You should not be a new convert. You should give evidence of being willing to accept supervision and to hold yourself accountable to the pastor or *director*. You should be in good physical, mental, and spiritual health.

Leadership Styles Required of Class Leaders

To be an effective *Class Leader* you must exercise a variety of leadership styles. During the gathering time, for example, you use strong relational skills to foster hospitality, while using organizational skills to maintain the schedule and the attention of the class. During the *reflection*, you exercise intuitive intelligence for discernment and empathy, practice active listening, and administer a defined process of watching over one another in love. Already, you have served as a facilitator, listener, caregiver, and manager.

During the study time, you become a teacher, but may approach the subject matter in a variety of ways, using a range of skills. Among the possible leadership styles appropriate for you as the teacher of an adult study session are: (1) presenter, (2) resource person, and (3) program *director*. The presenter conveys information as the primary speaker and then fields questions from the class members. The resource person relies on the group to explore the subject matter, usually outside of class; and then guides them in discovering a deeper level of understanding by providing clarification and information not otherwise available to the class. The teacher who functions primarily as a program *director* sets up and directs an active learning experience in which members exercise a variety of learning options, according to their interests and preferred learning styles. Ideally, you will learn how to move in and out of any of these three major instructional styles with ease, based upon the format of the curriculum and the subject matter.

Essential Leadership Skills and Shared Leadership

The class session requires you to fulfill at least two decidedly different leadership functions. For this reason, you will do well to draw upon the abilities of an assistant leader who can focus on either pastoral care or teaching. You may facilitate the *reflection* while a class member who is gifted as a teacher leads the instructional time. Shared leadership requires planning ahead and a measure of interpersonal compatibility.

You will find the companionship of a team approach supportive. With shared leadership, you can be away at times and remain confident that the class will be cared for. This makes the responsibility of leading less taxing. Moreover, the partnership functions as a self-correcting mechanism. The two leaders offer feedback and insight to each other as they seek to improve the quality of the class experience.

Job Description for a Class Leader

A *Class Leader* will:

1. Master the material in this manual and participate actively in laying the groundwork for, or contribute to maintaining, an effective system of discipleship in your local church.
2. Practice faithfulness to the covenant of your class and of your *band*.
3. Meet at least monthly with your *band*.
4. Communicate with the *director* or pastor promptly when any changes in practice, pastoral concerns, or issues related to group dynamics surface.
5. Facilitate *Class Meetings*.
6. Care for members of your class, either by telephone or in person, when they have special needs or are absent.
7. Work with the *director* and fellow *Class Leaders* to plan for and carry out quarterly meetings, Love Feasts, annual renewal weekends, parish communication, and testimonials within the local church.
8. Select, order, and distribute curriculum and facilitate study.
9. Recruit, welcome, and orient new members.

Job Description for Shared Leadership—Class Leader and Teacher

THE CLASS LEADER

Use the standard job description but delegate number eight. Join class members in contributing to the selection of curriculum.

THE TEACHER

1. Select, order, and distribute curriculum for study within the *Class Meeting*.
2. Prepare the lesson and conduct it.
3. Lead the class in evaluating course work and planning for future course work.

4

The Method of the Class Session

Using *This Day: A Wesleyan Way of Prayer* With a Small Group

As you prepare to organize your class, plan to have sufficient copies of the prayer book available so that all members can own and treasure their own copy. This book is to be a companion for many years, rather than a textbook for a course. Its primary function is to provide guidance for daily prayer and reflection on Scripture, in concert with thousands of other Christians who use this or a similar guide. In comparison with the wide range of other daily devotional guides available today, its distinctiveness lies in its origins and format derived from John Wesley's *Formulary for Prayer* (1735) and the *Book of Common Prayer*.

Each undated *daily office* is a part of a thirty-one-day cycle, based on the lunar calendar. (This system for daily use over the course of a month parallels the method for reading the Psalter that John Wesley outlined in his 1784 *Sunday Service* for American Methodists.) Class members are to plan to spend approximately twenty minutes each day in prayer. The reader will find the appropriate *daily office* by identifying the numerical day of the month. For example, on January 15 one would use Day 15; on March 12, one would use Day 12; and on Good Friday, one would turn to the special office prepared for Holy Week. Similarly, the reader will be able to locate the daily lectionary readings, including an appointed psalm, by determining which Sunday of the Christian year is coming next. A two-year cycle of lectionary readings can be located near the end of the prayer book as the *Daily Office Lectionary*. The thirty-one *daily offices* are to be used throughout each month of the year. There is no *daily office* for use on

Sundays, as members usually worship with the congregation, thereby fulfilling their usual practice of prayer and searching the Scriptures while observing the Lord's Day. In addition, *This Day: A Wesleyan Way of Prayer* provides special offices for feast days, each day of Holy Week, and the observance of the Ascension of the Lord. It suggests prayers for special occasions and particular needs, as well as an order for the Love Feast.

The original *Book of Common Prayer*, as used by Wesley and by the Church of England, was to be used in a chapel by a group of the faithful who would say the service aloud responsively and in unison. Although you may find reading the *daily office* aloud an unfamiliar way of praying, the daily devotional liturgy is designed to be recited either in the privacy of your room or with your household. Reading the office out loud enhances bodily participation in prayer, reinforces the beauty of the sacred texts, and enhances the believer's awareness of the church universal which participates together in the work of worship.

For this reason, the *daily office* is well suited for use within a quarterly meeting of the *society* or an assembly of all the classes within a congregation. It can also be used effectively in any team, committee, or study group in a local church in place of more typical devotional times. Using *This Day: A Wesleyan Way of Prayer* in this way will increase understanding and appreciation of the *Class Meeting* system throughout the parish.

Participants will need to be oriented to the prayer book, not only in terms of its organization and content, but also in terms of its use. Most Methodists have never participated in a complete *daily office* and never read their devotions aloud. It may be helpful to recite the *daily office* as a class. At first, members may find the private use of the office, and particularly the recitation of it, awkward and difficult.

You may choose to encourage participants to reach toward the goal of spending twenty minutes each day with the prayer book by initially attempting to devote ten minutes a day to using various parts of the office. This voluntary and abbreviated entry into what is to become a lifelong practice may reduce the temptation to feel burdened or enslaved by an unnatural form of devotion. It encourages growing into the practice through free experimentation. In this way the class may avoid the pitfall of becoming perfectionists in matters of piety or abandoning the discipline before it has the opportunity to become a way of life.

Members choose a particular time of day that they dedicate to spiritual formation, usually based on their alertness, the availability of time and space for solitude, and their ability to quiet themselves. Many find early morning the ideal time to devote to prayer. Before the activities of the day begin, they purify their intentions, focus their goals on seeking God's reign, and pray for guidance in light of the Scripture. Some prefer to take part of their lunch break for devotional time. Still others find it most beneficial to take their devotional time at the close of the day. After the work of the day is complete, they use their prayer time to gain perspective on what has taken place, to resolve their conflicts before God, to commend their work to God, and to quiet themselves for sleep by resting in God.

John Wesley advised spending time in prayer and self-examination both in the morning and before retiring at night. Regardless of the time of day, the purpose is to form a habit that will become as natural a practice as brushing one's teeth and as necessary to living the good life as eating a balanced diet. As the practice develops, it enables the disciple to "do everything for the glory of God," having spent quality time in loving attention to the Lord (1 Corinthians 10:31).

As the members complete the first month's experiment and begin to evaluate their progress, they may discover the reality that personality and age level differences affect the way people pray. As *Class Leader*, you need to be prepared to recommend a variety of prayer forms that may be helpful to those who find some aspects of the prescribed *daily office* cumbersome or unhelpful. (See Chapter 7 "Alternative *Forms of Prayer*.") These may be added to or occasionally substituted for the elements of the *daily office*. Moreover, class members may tailor a *daily office* to their own needs by creating a durable prayer card that outlines the pattern, taking care to include the essential elements.

The best way to introduce new *forms of prayer* and alternative offices is to demonstrate and practice them within the *Class Meeting*. Nevertheless, over the course of time, it would be well for you to encourage a return to the prescribed form and disciplined experimentation with standard forms. Often the *forms of prayer* that do not initially attract us or seem to fit our way of approaching God have something to teach us.

John Wesley used the *daily office* of the *Book of Common Prayer* in the privacy of his prayer room, spending an hour each day on his knees reciting the prescribed liturgy for the day and reading the appointed Scripture. His personal relationship with God was structured, informed, and nourished by the liturgy of the Church. Though Wesley often spent this early morning devotional time alone, it was not merely a form of introspection or subjective piety. When he prayed, he knelt in submission to God and in concert with the universal church and the saints who had gone before him. Without this time in prayer, Wesley believed he would rob God of God's time with him and undermine the spiritual foundation of his active ministry. Although the format and language of Wesley's prayer book was somewhat different from the contemporary guide, *This Day: A Wesleyan Way of Prayer* seeks to remain faithful to the intent, pattern, and content of the *daily office* that Wesley used.

Models for Daily Spiritual Exercises

John Wesley's Order for Morning Prayer

(to be used daily with the congregation)

Sentences of Scripture
The General Confession and Prayer for Pardon
Lord's Prayer
Gloria Patri
Psalm
Gloria Patri
Old Testament Lesson
Te Deum Laudamus (*We praise Thee, O God*)
New Testament Lesson
Psalm 100
Apostles' Creed
Prayers
Blessing

The Standard Order

The classic elements and approximate order of the *daily office* in *This Day: A Wesleyan Way of Prayer* follow:

Ascription of praise *(verse of Scripture)*
Collect *(opening prayer)*
Readings from the lectionary *(psalm, Old Testament, Gospel, New Testament)*
Forms of prayer *(confession, praise, thanksgiving, communion, petition, intercession, and blessing)*

An Alternative Pattern for Meditation and Prayer

(for those seeking a less formal guide to private devotions)

Centering prayer *(quieting one's self in the presence of God)*
Prayer for Illumination
Praying a psalm in sequence *(beginning with Psalm 1, reading one psalm per day)*
Silent prayer *(as inspired by the psalm)*
A reading from the Hebrew Scriptures or from the New Testament
    Epistles (based on the common lectionary, daily office lectionary, or a

sequential reading of the Bible)

The Gospel lesson for the coming Sunday *(read first for familiarity and again for hearing with understanding)*

Quiet *reflection* upon the passages *(as an act of listening for the word of God)*

Written *reflections (recording the Word as it is speaking to the worshiper that day, including a written commitment to respond faithfully)*

Prayers of thanksgiving and intercession for others

Closing blessing or prayer *(appropriate to the time of day, using a prayer suggested in* This Day: A Wesleyan Way of Prayer)

Minimalists will want to preserve both simplicity and integrity in their devotional plan (Matthew 6:1-15). Many balanced designs for daily spiritual formation can be created to suit the time frame, life stage, and temperament of the disciple. A full range of suggestions, appropriate to different learning and worship styles, can be found within this book. (See Chapter 7 "Alternative *Forms of Prayer.*") Any *daily office* for private or family prayer, however, should include each of the following elements:

A traditional prayer
Orderly Scripture reading
Self-examination
Praise, thanksgiving, intercession, and communion with God in silence

Wesleyan *Class Meetings:* No Solitary Christianity

The *Class Meeting* has always been a group of trusted friends who meet often over a long period of time. They become a community bound together by love for one another. Through the eyes of trusted members, each can see both themselves and the revelation of God more clearly than any could alone. The relationships forged within these classes, through prayer, confession, and study, prove to be among the disciples' most valued treasures. By way of mutual accountability before God, it is possible for Methodist Christians both to lead an active life in the world and to practice a godly lifestyle. Apart from such a pattern of personal discipline and mutual accountability, the evangelical experience of the gospel will fade and holy living will be reduced to frail optimism. Salvation will become a form of godliness lacking in power to save souls and redeem the world (2 Timothy 3:1-5).

In 1787 Wesley wrote, "I am not afraid that the people called Methodists should ever cease to exist either in Europe or America. But I am afraid, lest they should only exist as a dead sect, having the form of religion without the power. And this undoubtedly will be the case, unless they hold fast both the doctrine, spirit, and discipline with which they first set out" (*Thoughts Upon Methodism*, John Wesley in Welch, p. 205).

The Class Session: Practical Arrangements

The class session itself may be structured in a variety of ways. As *Class Leader*, you will need to determine the pattern that will work best within your local setting. Factors to consider include the day and time frame of the meeting, as well as the interests and gifts of the members. If your class meets as an adult Sunday school class for forty-five minutes each week, you should plan to spend twenty minutes in mutual accountability and twenty minutes in studying the Scriptures, leaving approximately five minutes for gathering, housekeeping, and a dismissal with blessing. If your class meets for sixty minutes, the session should include the singing of a hymn, the *reflection* or the question, "How is it with your soul?" and an extended time of group prayer, as well as Bible study. If your class meets for ninety minutes, at a time other than the Sunday school hour, the twenty minutes devoted to inquiring after one another's soul may be preceded by opening prayer and praise, probably including a hymn or song. In this case, a full hour can be given to study.

At least quarterly, hold a *Class Meeting* in which the Bible study curriculum is replaced with Scripture reading, testimonies or faith sharing, singing, and extemporaneous group prayer, as suggested by the order of service for the Wesleyan Love Feast.

In some cases, your class may be forced to meet less frequently than once a week. When disciples must choose to meet once a month, for example, extend the session to ninety minutes. This will allow for substantive study and thoughtful *Christian Conferencing*. All members can share their experience slowly and thoughtfully. The group can take the time to listen actively and respond to each speaker with discernment, without being pressured by other agenda. Prayer can be deep and healing. Whatever time frame is used, as leader you must begin and end on time, out of respect for members' schedules. This punctuality will underscore the seriousness of the discipline and protect the long-term commitment of the members to regular, sustained participation.

The Class Session Plan: Primary Model

Gathering
Opening *Prayer for Illumination*

Scripture Study
Reflection: "How Is It With Your Soul?"
Group Prayer
Dismissal With Blessing

As *Class Leader* you serve as a facilitator, timing the process and guiding the group through the essential elements of the session. You will open the session with prayer and facilitate study. The *reflection* follows.

Having listened deeply to the Scripture and heard the Word speaking plainly to them, the members' response to the *reflection* will be grounded in a biblical understanding of scriptural holiness. Your class will hold one another accountable and support one another in prayer. This plan encourages the group to engage in study in order both to understand the text and apply it to their own lives in the context of the *reflection*. By holding the *reflection* at the close of the class session, this time of mutual inquiry can be integral to the learning experience. It will be the intentional structure for transformational adult education.

A variety of session plans can be used, however, in support of the intent of twenty-first century Wesleyan *Class Meetings*. You may choose to experiment with several formats until your group finds one that best suits their time frame and personal needs. Some groups will begin with the *reflection* and then proceed to study. An expanded model, appropriate to a retreat setting, would include singing and testimonies or a group recitation of the *daily office*, with time for quiet *reflection* and journal entries. When a group reorganizes or adds new members, changing the order of the session may serve to refresh the process of mutual care and spiritual growth.

The Gathering

From the earliest days of the church, Christian hospitality has served as a vital expression of the outreaching love of God and a means of greeting one another in the peace of Christ. It continues to be a refuge for travelers, seekers, and those on the journey of faith today. While punctuality should be an expected component of group culture, the time of mutual greeting can be both warm and personal. The biblical "holy kiss" (2 Corinthians 13:12) and the Christian responsorial exchange, "The peace of the Lord be with you./**And also with you**," can become sacred tradition in the *Class Meeting* of today. This time of coming together, however, should take no more than five minutes.

The Opening Prayer

A variety of resources may be used to guide this important preparation for listening for the Word of God. The *Prayer for Illumination* may be an extemporaneous prayer led by you as *Class Leader* or by a different class member each time the group meets. The class may prefer to use a standard prayer recited by the group in unison. This prayer lends consistency and focus to the group's spiritual life and culture. You may choose to use one of these suggested prayers:

Lord, open our hearts and minds
by the power of your Holy Spirit,
that, as the Scriptures are read
and your Word proclaimed,
we may hear with joy what you say to us today.
Amen. (Service of Word and Table I, *United Methodist Hymnal*, p. 6)

O send out your light and your truth;
*   let them lead me;*
let them bring me to your holy hill
*   and to your dwelling. [Amen.]* (Psalm 43:3)

Spirit of God: We acknowledge our dependency upon you for life, insight, correction and redemption. Open our hearts and minds that we may hear your Word to us as we search the scriptures and learn together, in Jesus' name. Amen.

Scripture Study

As *Class Leader,* you will find a wide range of quality in printed adult study material. Use discretion in choosing material for use within the Wesleyan *Class Meetings*, in cooperation with the body responsible for designing and overseeing the educational ministries of your local church and in cooperation with your denominational publishing house. Always choose a curriculum that is closely related to the lectionary and can be readily adapted to the time frame available to your class. Among the recommended curricula are resources developed from *The International Lesson Series* and produced by respective denominational publishing houses. The lesson plan should include the following components:

1. Reading the text aloud
2. Exploring its original meaning
3. Discovering its message for today
4. Applying its message to the lives of group members

An alternative approach to the Bible study portion of the *Class Meeting* begins with exploring an issue or topic related to missions, social justice, ethics, or spiritual life. Ideally, the topic is one that the group selects on the basis of its relevance to the members or to the society at large, with the goal of studying all five major categories of subject matter over a defined period. Your class members may have read the study material in advance of the class session. During the class session, you and class members select passages from the text to read aloud, in order to ask searching questions and gain fresh insights. The study session ends with the group's stating how God's Word is calling the members into action (Romans 1:5-6).

Regardless of the approach to study, whether "text to life" or "life to text," the curriculum should provide responsible, scholarly background for you and class members. While in-depth study of biblical, theological, historical, spiritual, social, and ethical matters deepens discipleship and challenges superficial faith, the primary purpose of study within the *Class Meeting* is the transformation of the believers and the development of the mind of Christ in the community of God's people.

The Reflection

The *reflection* is a means of mutual accountability to the general rule of discipleship. It remains the centerpiece of the *Class Meeting*. Early Methodists were expected to be "entirely open" and "exhibit no kind of reserve," following the pattern of communal fellowship enjoyed by the Moravians whose *band* meetings modeled the quality of mutual accountability that Wesley expected of the *Class Meetings* (Watson, David Lowes, *The Early Methodist Class Meeting*, Nashville: Discipleship Resources, p. 81). Each member was to give a "straight-forward accounting of what had taken place during the previous week" (Watson, p. 97).

The Reflection Today

The inquiry or *reflection* can be handled differently today, without diminishing the effect. Each class must determine its own approach in a consensual manner, so that everyone feels safe and well prepared for participating voluntarily. Invest the necessary class time to design a *reflection* that no sincere disciple will consider invasive or judgmental. The following models offer suggestions:

Model 1:
Class Leader *Poses the Traditional Question to Each Member*

Post the group covenant or general rule of discipleship in large type so that all can see it. Instruct everyone to review it silently. Ask the question, "How is it with your soul?" Encourage each member to take approximately one minute to respond. Take no more than thirty seconds to offer feedback to each member before moving on to the next person. (*Advantages*: The standard for *reflection* and response is objective and consistent. All members participate actively. *Disadvantages*: This model does not allow for nonparticipation and assumes that the objective standard is both helpful and relevant at all times for all members. It is hurried.)

Model 2:
Voluntary Accountability Facilitated by Class Leader

Distribute cards on which the *General Rule* or class covenant is printed. Spend a moment in silence while members read the card and reflect on their faithfulness to the covenant. Invite members to share as they feel ready to do so, taking one minute to speak about the part of the covenant they are struggling with most or about which they would like to celebrate progress. Take thirty seconds for the group to respond to each person who shares.

Do not require that everyone share each time the class meets. If a member fails to share for more than two sessions, you should inquire privately after the well-being of that individual, seeking to encourage full participation. If the group completes its voluntary confession and celebration before the time allotted for the *reflection* has expired, return to any one whose concerns call for further care. Encourage group members to minister to one another both within and outside of class. (*Advantages*: More reticent or private members can avoid speaking while still participating. The *reflection* is based on an objective standard. The process is less rushed. *Disadvantage*: When one or more members fail to share, momentum in building a sense of community may be impaired and those who have accounted for themselves may feel unfairly exposed.)

Model 3:
The Reflection *as an Act of Worship*

Ask a member to read the group covenant or *General Rules* aloud. Lead a prayer that invites God to examine each member of the class. (Note: You may use a traditional prayer each time the class meets, such as "The Collect for Purity.")

Almighty God, to you all hearts are open, all desires known, and from you no secrets are hidden. Cleanse the thoughts of our hearts by the inspiration of your Holy Spirit, that we may perfectly love you, and worthily magnify your holy name, through Christ our Lord. Amen. (*United Methodist Book of Worship*, p. 447)

Spend some time in silence during which members review their week in the presence of God. Pray extemporaneously as a group, expressing thanks for those moments when each has experienced the *grace* of God at work in their lives or in the world at large. Move the group toward a time of confession and seeking guidance, correction, or healing. Encourage the class to respond to each member's prayer, with words such as, "Lord, in your mercy/**Hear our prayer.**" Close the time of prayerful examination by commending the class to God. You may pray extemporaneously or use a pattern of prayer, such as an adaptation of Jesus' words from the Cross: "Into your hands, O Lord, we commend our spirits, for you have redeemed us, O God of Truth." (See Luke 23:46.) (*Advantages:* Members participate voluntarily. The format is familiar to anyone who worships with a congregation. Accountability is chiefly to God, rather than to members of the class. *Disadvantages*: The objective standard of discipline may be lost and the sense of mutual accountability may be weakened.)

Model 4:
The Reflection *as a Report of Progress in Discipleship*

Ask your class to recite a contemporary rule of discipleship, such as: "To witness to Jesus Christ in the world, and to follow his teachings through acts of compassion, justice, worship, and devotion, under the guidance of the Holy Spirit" (Gayle Turner Watson, *Guide for Covenant Discipleship Groups* [Nashville: Discipleship Resources, 2000], p. 12). (*Note*: This form of the rule says nothing about avoiding evil. Some measure must be taken to integrate this aspect of the original *General Rules* into the class *reflection*. In order to provide a stimulus for considering how temptation has been handled, read a Scripture passage such as Romans 1:18-32 or Galatians 5:19-21. In addition, you may read aloud this Wesleyan *reflection:*

> Have I rejoiced with and for my neighbor in virtue or pleasure? Grieved with him in pain, or him in sin? Have I received his infirmities with pity, not anger? Have I thought or spoken unkindly of or to him? Have I revealed any evil of anyone, unless it was necessary to some particular good I had in view? Have I then done it with all the tenderness of phrase and manner consistent with that end? Have I anyway appeared to approve them that did otherwise? Has goodwill been, and appeared to be, the spring of all my actions toward others? Have I duly used intercession? Before, after, speaking to any? (Rueben Job, *Guide to Prayer for All God's People*, p. 145)

After quiet *reflection*, the group hears reports of each other's progress in observing one or more elements of the rule of discipleship: acts of witness, compassion, justice, or worship, including Holy Communion, private and family devotions, and fasting or abstinence. Your role is to facilitate the sharing, to see that everyone has an opportunity to speak, and to ensure that the group treats all aspects of the rule over the course of any given month of *Class Meetings*. (*Advantages*: This method preserves the objective standard and group accountability in a positive atmosphere, emphasizing progress in godliness rather than confession of sin. *Disadvantage*: Some people will not identify emotionally with the contemporary rule of discipleship. It may seem too general or overly complicated. Consider overcoming this problem by substituting the group's locally developed covenant, based on the *General Rules*.)

As in Wesley's day, a *Class Leader* must interpret the procedure for the *reflection* to any newcomer in advance. In order to assure regularity and preserve the integrity of the procedure, you will always guide the *reflection* as the *Class Leader*. Since this part of the *Class Meeting* system is both essential to maintaining discipline and the least popular aspect of the method, you must take care to introduce it in a manner that demonstrates respect for those who find it awkward. Do not proceed with a *reflection* until the class has reached consensus and the needs of all participants have been honored.

The Use of the *Reflection* in Extended Sessions

In retreat settings, in quarterly conferences, or at a Love Feast, for example, the pattern for the *reflection* might vary and be inspired by a specific theme or set of Scripture readings. An example follows. It is derived from and prepared to be used after one or more of these readings: Isaiah 12:3; 44:3; Psalm 63:1-4; 2 Corinthians 4:5-18; and John 7:37-39. The questions are asked during a period of silent *reflection* before a general prayer of confession.

> From what do I most need to be cleansed?
> What part of me is dry or weary?
> How open and thirsty for God am I?
> What did I receive from God this week?
> What of God have I passed on to others?
> For what nourishment of soul am I most thankful?

Prayer of General Confession

> We are weary and much in need of You, O God. Many tasks and a variety of interests, anxieties and passions distract us. In the busyness of our secular lives, we content ourselves with shallow waters, worn out ways, and half-truths. We have too often preferred superficial spirituality to the

deep waters of Your Spirit. We have not loved God with heart, soul, mind and strength, nor have we loved one another or our neighbors as we love ourselves. We have loved lesser gods and spent our days in ways that waste sacred time. Rarely have we served to refresh and renew the earth or its people. Forgive us and transform us, O Lord, for the sake of Your Peace. Fill us that we may thrive in the fullness of Your Presence among us. Grant that, through Christ, we may serve with You to heal and redeem. We pray in Jesus' name. Amen.

IN SUMMARY: THE FUNCTION OF THE *REFLECTION*

The purpose of accountability in the *Class Meeting* is not to foster enjoyable social relationships among peers but to encourage growth in spiritual and moral maturity. The *reflection* is not an inquiry after the physical or emotional health of friends and neighbors. The goal of the *reflection* is that the highest good may be known and incorporated into the daily lives of men and women called to be disciples of Christ. The *Class Meeting* is, therefore, *not a self-help or support group*. It is not a form of group counseling. Unlike any other setting, the *Class Meeting* serves to encourage, invite, and sustain the pursuit of holiness, so that the image of God may be restored within the believer and the presence of Christ may be seen in the world through the church.

By limiting the format of the *reflection*, both in content and in time frame, you as *Class Leader* preserve its integrity and simplicity. At the same time, care in focusing the group process avoids the pitfalls of exposing people to scrutiny or confession that they may later regret. To be effective, you must guide the process of mutual examination so as to protect confidences that would better be shared within the context of family, pastoral, or other professional therapeutic relationships.

Group Prayer

Prayer with others offers an experience of divine power and presence that is entirely different from the experience of God that comes in solitude. Matthew's Gospel reports Jesus' promise to meet with believers following his death and resurrection: "For where two or three are gathered in my name I am there among them." The early church so valued these meetings that they assembled to pray together daily (Acts 2:42). This portion of class time should not be rushed. It may be the most important aspect of the class session.

Usually, after inviting members to gather the needs and concerns of their peers and present them before God as they feel moved to do so, you will open the time of prayer. Typically, you will sense when the class has finished praying and you will lead in the Lord's Prayer. Specific forms of group prayer deserve thoughtful use.

INTERCESSION

Intercessory prayer for someone present in the room, particularly when one can touch the person while praying for them, provides for discernment and inspired speech, prophetic ministry, and the quickening of faith in the beneficiary as well as in those praying. The culture and the personalities within your class will influence the way members choose to pray for one another. Some groups so value the laying on of hands during intercessory prayer that when this is not done, members feels cheated or neglectful. In another setting, anything more than a general prayer of intercession from the prayer book will feel overly intimate. Some groups prefer silent intercession, followed by the Lord's Prayer, rather than extemporaneous group prayer. You will need to experiment with a variety of approaches, carefully introducing each approach and never assuming that everyone will be comfortable with a particular way to pray for others.

DEVELOPING THE INTUITIVE VOICE IN PRAYER

Listening actively and deeply is vital to learning to pray with and for others extemporaneously. The collective intelligence of the class, as inspired by divine love, can perceive the spoken or unspoken needs, joys, and longings of the members. While empathy requires the ability to feel with another, effective intercessory prayer requires intuition, analytical thought, being present in compassion and humility, and knowing when to touch and when to remain respectful of the privacy of the other. It requires self-emptying and silence. God's love "poured into our hearts through the Holy Spirit that has been given to us" breathes hope and faith into the corporate work of active and prayerful listening (Romans 5:5). Clearly, all members have a role to play in hearing how the Spirit prays for the other and then articulating that Divine Voice so as to enliven the faith of those who watch and pray (Romans 8:26-27).

Some members will be gifted for leading this kind of prayer. Others will be most effective in silence. The goal is to allow the Spirit to pray through the believers, so that the class prays according to the will of God (Matthew 18:19-20; John 14:12-14; James 5:13-16).

RESPONSORIAL PRAYER

Responsorial prayer provides yet another way of engaging a class in active verbal prayer. This prayer form offers the group a refrain by which to respond to a standard call to prayer. For example, you may say, "I will lead us in a series of petitions, after each of which I will say, 'Lord, hear our prayer'; and you will respond, '**And let our cry come unto Thee.**'"

Consider using this call/response from the Lord's Prayer: "Thy Kingdom come/ **On earth as in heaven.**" Or try, "Search us and know us, O God/**And lead us in the way that leads to life.**" A similar call/response format can be sung: "This is our prayer/ **This is our prayer, O Lord.**" Only the boundaries of prayerful imagination limit the variety of ways this approach to the use of the language of prayer can serve to unite and empower contemporary disciples of Christ.

DISMISSAL WITH BLESSING

The class session closes with a benediction. Use a classic Christian blessing taken from *This Day: A Wesleyan Way of Prayer* or from Scripture (2 Corinthians 13:13; Galatians 6:18; Philippians 4:23). A brief responsorial benediction may be used, such as "The Peace of the Lord be with you/ **And also with you.**" When the class meets for ninety minutes, the dismissal may include a hymn of discipleship or a sung benediction. This breaks the pattern of you as *Class Leader* always giving the benediction. It encourages the priesthood of all believers to bless one another.

5

Theology and the Method of Methodism in the Twenty-first Century

The Theology of Prayer and Spiritual Formation: Thinking About God

The understanding of God that seekers and disciples take to the work of prayer and spiritual formation deeply influences both our approach and the results we obtain. Even though our concept of God does not alter God, it alters what we perceive and what we pursue. It both limits and enhances our spiritual life. It shapes every aspect of who we become and what we do over the course of the life span.

Theology matters. While it is an ancient discipline, its work is never finished. Because circumstances change, cultures shift, and the slow, painful evolutionary process evident in the physical world also occurs in the history of ideas, humanity's understanding of God is a dynamic process. John and Charles Wesley made significant contributions to the theology of their Anglican heritage. While their work adopted the Articles of Religion honored by the Church of England, their preaching, teaching, and hymnody addressed theological and practical religious issues of the day. It emphasized new birth, assurance, and Christian perfection in the context of an evangelical revival that swept all of Great Britain, the United States, and Canada. As the movement spread around the world and met people of differing cultures, Methodists coached and occasionally led the evolution of religion and the development of the international search for God.

The Theological Task Today

The theology of the traditional doctrine and prayers that the Wesley brothers used has been preserved and still shapes our devotional life today. The way we understand God, ourselves, and our relationship with God has shifted significantly over the three centuries that separate us from the beginning of their remarkable lives. In our effort to determine how we think about matters of faith, we consider the Scriptures of the Old and New Testaments; the tradition or doctrines and teachings of the Christian church; the history of ideas; current knowledge; and our own thoughts, intuitions, information, and direct experiences of God. Moreover, we rely on the active presence of God with us by the Holy Spirit to illumine our souls and enlighten our understanding. (See Jeremiah 31:31-34; Mark 1:7-8; Luke 24:49; Acts 2:1-21; John 14:15-26.)

Theology is a process in which everyone participates, either consciously or unconsciously. The more actively we participate in this dynamic process of coming together to reflect and going out to serve, the more likely we are to experience personal progress and contribute to the well-being of others. In "doing" theology, we intentionally think and act with God, whether alone or with others.

Doing Theology Within the *Class Meeting* System

The daily changes that inevitably occur as people reflect on their lives in the context of good and evil, God and nature, religion and science, life and death, and increasing interaction between East and West have spawned theological openness and an appreciation for education among Methodists. The time devoted to applying the biblical message to contemporary concerns and circumstances in each *Class Meeting* will be one of the most important aspects of the spiritual formation process. This element of the educational method will force the work of theology on all participants and challenge the safety of static thinking. It is the revelation of God in Jesus, however, that perpetually brings us together and focuses our perceptions.

As we gather, we give our attention to Christ Jesus, our Lord. As if sitting at the feet of Jesus who continues to share all that he knows of God with us, our understanding grows while we pray, think, share, and study the Scriptures together (Matthew 5:1-2; John 15:15). To the extent that we yield our minds to the teaching of Jesus and the apostles, we find ourselves bound together with God and one another. The community that is formed in this process purifies us, revitalizes our inmost selves, refreshes us physically, and empowers us with joy and peace. In this way, theology becomes an active part of our relationship with God, much as understanding a spouse, a child, or a friend deepens our ability to love them well.

At the same time that we are bound together in Christian love, we remain separate individuals with various gifts, perspectives, and experience. Like the ebb and flow of the tide, our coming together and our parting provides continual renewal of both the individuals and the group. As we face inward toward our Master Teacher, Jesus, and see through him to his God; so then he sends us out into the towns and villages to meet the world in peace and to discover the Christ in neighbors and strangers (Matthew 28:19-20). When we return, we rejoice in our privilege of communion together with God (Luke 10:1-20).

In this way, our faith gains perspective and our vision of God transcends private experience and understanding. The God we seek, after all, lives and breathes in people of every age, nation, race, and tradition in towns and villages we will never enter, while remaining altogether Spirit and greater than anything human or otherwise material. Theological reflection leads us to doubt our prejudices and search for the truth that lies beyond our previous perceptions. It forces fresh expressions of God through us and sustains hope in the midst of doubt and danger.

The Theology Behind Traditional Prayer

Biblical prayer indicates that God is a personal being with whom one has a relationship. Just as responsible parents hear and respond to the requests and needs of their children, so God gives what is good to those who ask (Matthew 7:7-11). The language of traditional prayer assumes that God hears and answers the petitions of God's people and receives honor through faithful expressions of praise and thanksgiving. Moreover, most believers expect that their sins are truly forgiven only after they confess their sin to God and ask for divine forgiveness.

The general understanding is that God resides in the heavens, above the earth. Thus, supplicants lift up holy hands unto the Lord above as their prayers rise to God. This spatial understanding of the relationship between God and humanity, and between the prayers of the people and the Lord of heaven and earth, is deeply ingrained in religious life and its vocabulary.

People will find traditional prayer, as offered in *This Day: A Wesleyan Way of Prayer*, more or less helpful, depending partly on their theology. Twenty-first century scientifically educated seekers often find themselves having to translate the language of prayer, like persons learning to converse in a second language. It may be helpful to use a variety of non-traditional images and metaphors, in conjunction with the traditional resources, as means of meditation and prayer. (See Chapter 7 "Alternative *Forms of Prayer.*")

Diversity and the Theology Behind the Language of Prayer

While God is Spirit and everywhere available, people approach God through a wide range of theological prisms. Many adults think about God in terms they learned in childhood. Their theological language and imagery remain literal and concrete. The *anthropomorphic* metaphors of the Bible provide them comfort and ease of access to God. At the same time, fellow members of the same class may find references to God's arms, hearing, walking, sight, will, or fatherhood offensive. Others resist using terms of power, such as "King" or "Lord." Some exclude gender-specific references to God from their religious vocabulary. Still others, having found their way through an iconoclastic or demythologizing phase of theological and spiritual wandering, can enjoy the poetic power of this symbolic language without deriving their theology from it. They participate in God through the *anthropomorphic* world of thought, as if worshiping before an icon or praying through an illumined stained glass window. They enjoy the freedom of childlike faith, without being childish in their thinking. They know that "for now we see as in a mirror, dimly, but then we will see face to face" (1 Corinthians 13:12a).

Many contemporary Methodists have been so alienated by the institutional church or the history of religion that they reject traditional theological categories altogether and approach God as an amorphous "higher power" or "force." They prize their freedom from doctrinal definitions of God and may protest the requirement of biblical study or traditional prayer. Although God is more than a personal guardian angel or private power source, if a class member has found strength from such an approach to God or to wellness, then the *Class Leader* must honor the other's spiritual path. If, for example, one of the Twelve Step programs has opened the seeker to the church, that doorway to faith has served a vital function and must not be undermined. The role of theological reflection and biblical study is to inform rather than to judge. One of the functions of the class is to invite community and to lead the seeker into an appreciation for other perspectives, names for God, experiences of *grace*, and theological categories.

A few mystics find their way into small groups, hoping for company among fellow seekers. They often bring gifts of illumination and joy, as well as acquaintance with the dark side of the soul. Theirs may be an experience of God as Lover. For them, God is both more than any thing (Nothing) and immediately present. Their God is light and love. They have tasted God's glory, as if by sensory awareness, and have been forever changed by their firsthand experience of the divine. They may be among the most appreciative of the *daily office*, readily following it as a path to contemplation. They may also value a variety of art forms that aid worship and express the ineffable beauty of divine holiness. While ecstatic union with God may be their goal, these usually introspective personalities sometimes offer their treasured experience and their acute listening skills to others, thereby enhancing the Christian community in which they participate.

Some adults come to the practice of faith by way of science or philosophy. While they may have been raised in the church, their primary point of reference may be from outside the church. They approach God intellectually and rely on reason to verify their experience of *grace*. They relate better to those who worship God in Spirit and in truth, than to those who see God as the Lover of their souls or the Everlasting Arms. A philosophical image of God, such as First Principle, Prime Mover, Ground of Being, or Source, may work best for them. They think and move in concert with the revelation to Moses on Mount Sinai when YHWH said to the prophet, "You shall say to the Israelites, 'I AM has sent me to you' " (Exodus 3:14). They maintain respect for the mystery of God, both in their theology and in their practice of the faith, while claiming the privilege of knowing God intimately enough to call God by name. They contribute to theological study by way of their searching questions and their critical thinking. They may, however, struggle to feel comfortable with the literal, mystical, emotional, or relational theology of other group members. Moreover, they may find the ritual of saying the *daily office* a practice that lacks firm grounding in reality as they know it. It may feel to them like a form without transformational power.

Some find all liturgy, activity, and conversation distracting. They require solitude and often prefer to find it in nature. They sense the mystery beyond the horizon or in the complexity of creation, but find traditional language about God irrelevant.

Quiet souls may have difficulty finding words by which to articulate their beliefs. They appreciate the fact that others speak and write about their faith easily. They prefer, however, to witness to their faith through deeds of mercy and acts of justice. They think of God best without language. They use their ability to listen, their hands, their sweat, and their skills as prayer forms. Prayer is most real for them while serving others. They feel closest to God when helping someone else. The effective *Class Leader* seeks to be conversant with all of these perspectives and expressions of faith, respecting each theological perspective to the extent that it supports men and women in their search for God.

The *Class Leader's* Theological Function

As a *Class Leader*, it will be important for you to be self-aware. With which of these perspectives of God do you identify? Which of these irritates you or is least helpful to you? Which one intrigues you, though you find it unfamiliar? Which seems to dominate the perspective of *This Day: A Wesleyan Way of Prayer*? By answering these questions clearly and honestly before attempting to lead a class, you prepare yourself to avoid undermining someone else's pursuit of God and godliness. At the same time, you recognize your own gifts and limitations, and the bias of the tradition.

Historically, the majority of Methodists have approached God through their emotions. They relate to God as love and enjoy expressing their feelings toward God in hymns, stories, extemporaneous prayer, and conversation. As *Class Leader*, you will do well, regardless of your personal preferences, to incorporate these ways of being with God into the majority of session plans.

Thinking About Contemporary Prayer

Prayer that is directed toward God as the personification of all that is good and true, creative, and life-giving opens the seeker to the sacred and creates access to the Essence of Life. The act of prayer awakens us to God-with-us and shows us who we are as persons created in the image of God. Paul writes:

> But when one turns to the Lord, the veil is removed. Now the Lord is the Spirit, and where the Spirit of the Lord is, there is freedom. And all of us, with unveiled faces, seeing the glory of the Lord as though reflected in a mirror, are being transformed into the same image from one degree of glory to another; for this comes from the Lord, the Spirit. (2 Corinthians 3:16-18)

Through prayer, we begin to consciously accept the life of God in us and our vocation as those who carry *Being* within us (1 Corinthians 3:16; Luke 1:26-35). Prayer has the potential to transform our approach to ourselves, to the business of life, and to others.

Prayer can be the soul's way of loving and enjoying God, savoring the privilege of spiritual awareness, and living in the moment. It can purify our hearts, our wills, our thoughts, and the inmost parts of our selves. Prayer can be a way of affirming what we know to be true, claiming it consciously, and making it our way of life, leading us into an eschatological experience of the kingdom of God here and now. When we pray in concert with the faithful everywhere, especially in daily recitation of the Lord's Prayer, we speak our faith aloud and the words create an awareness of God among us because they are the Word of God.

Ultimately, prayer can help us become the meek of the earth, humbled as we are by our inability to pray well. If we are patient and sufficiently frustrated with ourselves, our limitations, and the needs around us, we may experience God praying through us. As Paul promised:

> Likewise the Spirit helps us in our weakness; for we do not know how to pray as we ought, but that very Spirit intercedes with sighs too deep for words. And God, who searches the heart, knows what is the mind of the Spirit, because the Spirit intercedes for the saints accoding to the will of God." (Romans 8:26-27)

When the Spirit of God prays through us, we open our souls to what many have called the "mind of Christ," setting our own agendas and values aside (1 Corinthians 2:16).

In the end, as at the beginning, God is; and we find rest in God. We enter silence and somehow find a contentment beyond language or reason, beyond spatial or sensory awareness, and beyond ourselves. With the psalmist we can pray,

> O LORD, my heart is not lifted up, my eyes are not raised too high;
> I do not occupy myself with things too great and too marvelous for
>   me.
> But I have calmed and quieted my soul, like a child quieted at its
>   mother's breast; like a child that is quieted is my soul.
>
> O Israel, hope in the LORD from this time forth and for evermore.
>   (Psalm 131 RSV)

Out of this experience of Spirit-led prayer, the words attributed to Jesus take on fresh meaning: "Come to me, all you that are weary and are carrying heavy burdens, and I will give you rest. Take my yoke upon you, and learn from me; for I am gentle and humble in heart, and you will find rest for your souls. For my yoke is easy, and my burden is light" (Matthew 11:28-30).

Intercessory Prayer as God's Work Among Us

Prayer for others, guided by compassion and offered in surrender and trust toward God, becomes a means of divine agency. That is to say, God works through this form of prayer, as we allow the creative, life-sustaining, and redeeming reality of God to shape our perspective on the people for whom we pray. We become channels of *grace*.

It may help to visualize a triangle. Imagine Christ, his life offered for us and our salvation, signified by a cross at the center of the triangle. Understand God as denoted by the apex of the triangle. A second point of the triangle represents the person for whom you pray. You sit, stand, or prostrate yourself at the third point. Through prayer, while holding the other for whom you intercede in your thoughts, you gain direct access to God through the faith of Jesus and in his name. By connecting with God and with the other, you release the power of faithful love.

There is no greater healing or reconciling power in all the world. People do not control it or define it. We simply connect with it on behalf of others. Our prayer expresses the divine nature and offers God's *grace* to the other. Long experience verifies the power of praying for others.

The reality behind intercessory prayer remains constant in private, group, and public prayer. The way people experience it in each of these settings, however, may differ. When we pray for someone else while alone, we may experience deep and silent intimacy with God. When we pray in a small group or with one other person, the dynamics of the relationship are more immediate than they are when we pray for others at a distance. Joining hands or practicing the laying on of hands can make prayer both physical and sensory. We may feel an inner warmth or power flowing through us. Often we sense the presence of the Lord with us. We "discern what is the will of God—what is good and acceptable and perfect" (Romans 12:2).

When we gather with other believers to intercede for the world, we lift our hearts toward God in concert with the global church. We release our faith and our burdens, joining hearts and minds with the assembly of believers in affirming God's authority to save us and help us. Our cries, though often silent, are united with those of all others who pray with us that day. It is as if our concert of prayer expresses with groans and "sighs too deep for words" the birth pangs of a new age (Romans 8:18-26). In this way, we submit to the instruction and blessing of the apostle, "Do not worry about anything, but in everything by prayer and supplication with thanksgiving let your requests be made known to God. And the peace of God, which surpasses all understanding, will guard your hearts and your minds in Christ Jesus" (Philippians 4:6-7; see also 1 Thessalonians 5:17).

Thinking About God in the Midst of the Class Meeting

The early church testified to their experience by placing on the lips of Jesus these words: "Where two or three are gathered in my name, I am there among them" (Matthew 18:20). Like our Jewish predecessors who carried the ark of the covenant with them as a sign of God's going before them whenever they moved, so we depend upon the presence of God with us. We know that we cannot save ourselves from our persistent inclination to lust, greed, power, pride, overindulgence, anger, resentment, or materialism. We are forever inclined toward self-centeredness and behavior that undermines our self-respect, inner peace, relationships with others, and communion with God. Apart from the *grace* of God-with-us and the active guidance of the Spirit, God's Word, and those more experienced in the way of salvation than we are, we will falter. God's presence in the gathered church becomes the vital link, the voice, the outstretched hand that prevents us from falling into sin.

The community into which we are baptized, and into which we have been called as disciples of Jesus, is a redemptive communion with God and others like ourselves. Apart from this bond of fellowship, the Christian life loses its meaning and its power. Salvation becomes a merely private pursuit of perfection or of life beyond death, rather than participation in the reign of God on earth as it is in heaven. When believers hold one another accountable and nurture one another, however, their community becomes a living demonstration of God's saving power in the world today. As God's love is "poured into our hearts through the Holy Spirit that has been given to us," God proves the amazing reality of the Good News, "The time is fulfilled, and the kingdom of God has come near" (Romans 5:5; Mark 1:14).

Thinking About the Soul and Its Journey Toward God

Ultimately the journey of spiritual formation is about God and not about us. It is a journey of the soul toward God and in God. For this reason, it matters which God we seek. What we believe about God directly affects what we become. The truly godly life is manifest, however, when it can be seen by others that the Holy Spirit rests on us, as it did on Simeon (Luke 2:25). It proves itself when, with Mary, we say, "Let it be with me according to your word" (Luke 1:38b), or, with Jesus, "Into your hands I commend my spirit" (Luke 23:46). All our efforts to think, pray, and live according to God's law merely keep us ready to serve as available vessels of the Spirit.

When we ask, "How is it with your soul?" we inquire after the essential self. In referring to the "soul," we search for that part of the human being that is morally and emotionally accountable to God, at the conscious, preconscious, and unconscious levels. We seek to examine all aspects of ourselves in the light of the glory of God revealed in Christ Jesus our Lord.

We do so on the basis of profound respect for God as the Source of our life and as the One to whom we must submit ourselves in life and in death. With our Hebrew forebears we acknowledge that the whole person, including our physical being, belongs to God and comes from divine initiative. Ultimately, our responsibility before God as the people of God includes stewardship of mind, body, spirit, psyche, time, relationships, and possessions within the context of human community.

The state of any individual soul affects all others. For this reason, the effective *Class Leader* recognizes the complex interrelatedness of the class members. Moreover, the *Class Leader* will, over time, guide the class in exploring the many aspects of who they are. Their physical, emotional, relational, and spiritual wellness will all come under care as the *Class Leader* poses the primary Wesleyan question, "How is it with your soul?"

A class member who is emotionally distressed by depression, or who is physically ill, may not be able to speak clearly about the depths of self. Even the usual practice of the means of *grace* may be difficult. Anyone who is not well in mind or body may experience the usual practices of the faith as nothing more than empty ritual. Effective care of these souls will take the form of compassion, prayer, and patience, rather than examination or discipline.

On the other hand, some healthy people who live active lives confess that they are aware of at least two levels of self that coexist: (1) the physical, intellectual, and emotional self which responds to its environment; and (2) the unchanging depths of self which rests in God. Some speak of the two poles of the inner and outer self. Frequently, dreams or spontaneous reactions to others, including body language, reveal aspects of the soul that are not otherwise apparent. Members of a class may find the active listening and faithful friendship of their companions a vital source of self-awareness and means of guidance. Friends in faith can help us see ourselves more clearly. They can show us our blind spots and deepen our self-understanding.

The Human Condition and Lifelong Discipleship: The Theology of Confession

Methodists are pragmatists. Our practice of the Christian faith is not so much about correct doctrine as it is about what works. John Wesley described the movement in this way:

> The points we chiefly insisted upon were four: First, that orthodoxy, or right opinions, is, at best, but a very slender part of religion, if it can be allowed to be any part of it at all; that neither does religion consist in negatives, in bare harmlessness of any kind; nor merely in externals, in

doing good, or using the means of grace, in works of piety (so called) or of charity; that it is nothing short of, or different from, "the mind that was in Christ;" the image of God stamped upon the heart; inward righteousness, attended with the peace of God; and "joy in the Holy Ghost." Secondly, that the only way under heaven to this religion is, to "repent and believe the Gospel;" or (as the Apostle words it) "repentance toward God, and faith in our Lord Jesus Christ." Thirdly, that by this faith, "he that worketh not, but believeth on him that justifieth the ungodly, is justified freely by his grace, through the redemption which is in Jesus Christ." And, lastly, that "being justified by faith," we taste of the heaven to which we are going; we are holy and happy; we tread down sin and fear, and "sit in heavenly places with Christ Jesus." ("Letters to a Member of the Society" in vol. 12 *The Works of John Wesley*, ed. Thomas Jackson, p. 289)

Methodists are interested in learning a way of life that increasingly fulfills Jesus' vision of the blessed people of God (Matthew 5:1-16). John Wesley wrote, "Always remember the essence of Christian holiness is simplicity and purity: one design, one desire: entire devotion to God" (Rueben Job, Norman Shawchuck, *A Guide to Prayer for Ministers and Other Servants* [Nashville: Upper Room Books, 1983], p. 368). We want to be the salt of the earth and light shining as from a lamp in the midst of a dark world (Matthew 5:13-16). We find that while faith brings assurance of a right relationship with God, a right relationship with self and others requires ongoing attention to God and constant discipline of our natural inclinations.

Although we may well be at peace today, tomorrow will bring new challenges. As much as we remember when we were lost and then rescued by amazing *grace*; we also know that some part of ourselves remains in need of redemption. On another day, we may again need pardon and mercy. Moreover, we recognize that our culture and economy engage us in unjust systems, making us guilty of corporate sin. More often than not, we passively cooperate with evil disguised as expediency, necessity, or prosperity. The mutual confession that we practice in the *Class Meeting* may be the most authentic form of repentance and justifying *grace* available to us. It is both a practical means of reaffirming our faith in the face of temptation and compromise and a way of accessing the transformational power of God.

Thinking About the *Class Meeting* in Relationship to the Church

The historical context of the Wesleyan movement within the Anglican Church may provide the most helpful means of interpreting the relationship between the *Class Meeting* and the larger church today. The early Methodists, with their societies, stewards, *bands, Class Leaders,* and classes, understood themselves to be part of a renewal movement within the established Church of England. Quakers, Presbyterians, and other dissenters were welcomed but encouraged to remain faithful to their own denominations, beliefs, and practices. So also today, the *Class Meeting* system is a connection of Methodists who take their membership in the Body of Christ seriously enough to hold one another accountable to their vows. They watch over one another in love, practice private prayer and Scripture study, and serve others in acts of mercy throughout the week. Still, their life as Christians would be incomplete without the fellowship, sacraments, ministries, and celebrations of the larger church. It is as if the *Class Meeting* is a family unit within the community of God's people. It is both its most essential unit and, at the same time, dependent upon the full functioning and governance of the universal church.

While not all Methodists will pursue the discipline of the *Class Meeting,* all members of classes will participate fully in the broader life of their congregation, their denomination, and the ecumenical church. Moreover, those who are members of a class will likely be the most active servant leaders and the most effective in nurturing new converts and newcomers to the faith community. They know that their participation in the class is not an end but a means. It provides the nurture necessary to active ministry. It serves as a means of spiritual renewal and reform within the larger church.

Tragically, since the late nineteenth century, the Methodist movement has been institutionalized in Europe, Great Britain, and North America and is in need of revival. The ministry of the laity and lay pastors, including *Class Meetings,* diminished with the establishment of station churches, parsonages, and long-term pastorates. With the decline of *Class Meetings* came a sharp decline in the discipline and method of Methodism. Members became churchgoers, rather than disciples. Being a Methodist became as much a matter of social identity as a means of salvation. The purpose and function of many local ministries was reduced to providing for the religious expectations of their member and nonmember constituencies. The energy of the local church was focused on conserving the culture of the community, celebrating the sacraments, performing rites of passage, comforting the afflicted, and paying the bills. The spreading of scriptural holiness across the land became a matter of archival note, rather than a driving passion. Without the renewal of Christian discipline and community life in the early twenty-first century, Methodism will become a relic of the past. With a resurgence of spiritual discipline, however, the biblical gathering of disciples as if at the feet of Jesus will become the means of renewal that the church so desperately needs today.

6

Planning for Group Diversity

Respecting Diversity

Just as one size of shoes does not fit all, one method of spiritual practice will not nourish all souls. Temperament, life stage, socioeconomic background, ethnicity, birth order, educational level, and preferred learning style all shape the individual's choice of spiritual path. Creating a welcoming environment for all people means offering acceptance without demanding conformity. It also requires the *Class Leader* to have an alert mind prepared to recognize the different needs and spiritual gifts of the individuals who join the *Class Meeting*.

By listening deeply to people who we do not immediately understand, we enter momentarily into the other's world and experience. We pause in wonder at the way they perceive life. When we hold our tongues and make the effort to leap over conceptual barriers, we can explore new fields of vision and dare to trust the validity of an alternative approach to God. We withhold judgment and resist the temptation to persuade others to become like us. We discover our biases, ignorance, and myopia in matters of faith. Having done so, we can reclaim our own perspective with greater humility, having grown through our relationship with people different from ourselves.

Understanding the Spiritual Bias of the Wesleyan *Class Meeting*

The Wesleyan *Class Meeting* is a clearly evangelical approach to spiritual formation that is focused on personal transformation. It relies heavily on the individual's experience of converting *grace*. At its core is a "heart strangely warmed." Its goal is holiness of heart and life. John Wesley wrote:

> By salvation I mean, not barely, according to the vulgar notion, deliverance from hell or going to heaven, but a present deliverance from sin; a restoration of the soul to its primitive health, its original purity; a recovery of the divine nature; the renewal of our souls after the image of God.... True religion is the loving of God with all our heart, and our neighbor as ourselves; and in that love abstaining from all evil and doing all possible good to all. ("A Farther Appeal to Men of Reason and Religion in Part 1," *The Works of John Wesley,* Vol. 11, ed. Gerald R. Cragg [Nashville: Abingdon Press, 1975], p. 106)

The culture and method of Methodism is relational. It assumes that people who are genuine disciples of Christ will benefit from and choose community as the setting in which they practice lifelong faithfulness. Wesley put it this way: " 'Holy solitaries' is a phrase no more consistent with the gospel than holy adulterers. The gospel of Christ knows of no religion, but social; no holiness but social holiness" ("Preface, Hymns, and Sacred Poems" in *The Works of John Wesley*, ed. Thomas Jackson, 14:321 [London: Wesleyan Methodist Book Room, 1872]).

This set of assumptions, values, and approaches to spiritual formation represents the spiritual path of choice for a significant segment of any Christian community. It fits affective learners well. These people learn best through their felt experiences. They prefer to learn through conversation and group *reflection*. Those who will most readily invest in the Wesleyan *Class Meeting* trust their feelings more than their theories, the familiar more readily than the "Cloud of Unknowing," and personal conversion in the context of a relationship with God over humanitarianism.

How the Wesleyan *Class Meeting* Can Benefit Those Who Might Not Seem to Fit

The Wesleyan *Class Meeting* can provide a healthy balance for people who are neither affective nor relational in their personality types and preferred learning style. Those who enjoy solitude and introspection or mystical awareness of God as their primary spiritual path can benefit from keeping company with more extroverted people. While they may be uncomfortable with an emphasis on a "personal relationship with God," as espoused by those who see God as a heavenly Parent or Friend, if their more traditional peers can respect a less personalized understanding of God, these atypical Methodists may adapt well to the warmth of the *Class*

Meeting experience. The joy of Christian fellowship can provide the emotional nourishment they need, as well as the challenge to see themselves and others differently. It will, however, be uncomfortable for them to participate on a regular basis in a Wesleyan *Class Meeting*, if the affective/relational religious style is presented as the normative approach to God. Quiet meditation can be more effective for some than conversation or self-revealing confession.

The Wesleyan *Class Meeting* may also prove frustrating for those who prefer active service as their primary spiritual path. These kinetic and sensory learners, people who learn and grow by doing, will find the time and energy spent in self-examination and sharing unproductive. In the end, however, by keeping company with the other class members, they may discover that the tasks they accomplish or the service they perform is only a path of approach to God and not, in itself, communion with God. They may become open to the presence of God within the class and in the people they serve, in part as a result of spending time with more verbal, cognitive, affective, and intuitive disciples of Christ.

Unless the study portion of the class is well developed, the Wesleyan *Class Meeting* will leave those who approach God primarily through the intellect feeling unfulfilled. While the ten to twenty minutes set aside for tending the souls of a dozen people in a *Class Meeting* may seem insufficient to most affective learners, it may seem tedious to those who need to think their way to godliness. The more rational believers within the class may, however, learn through their participation in the class simply to be with God and one another. They may become more self-aware. Their ability to empathize with people whom they may never have spent time with before may grow. Moreover, they may find themselves expressing their faith in ways that they previously found embarrassing.

Building Strength Through Diversity

If handled with care, a heterogeneous membership can discover the strength that comes from diversity. Class members will grow in faith and understanding as they never would have had they restricted themselves to the comfortable company of those like themselves.

We propose, therefore, to address the challenge of diversity by welcoming it and planning for it. We affirm that affective learners need cognitive, sensory/kinetic, and mystical companions. We claim kinship with those who learn by doing and put their faith into action before they put it into words. We value quiet and silence in our private prayer, study, and *reflection* as guided by *This Day: A Wesleyan Way of Prayer*. We intend to use high quality adult education material and to encourage excellence in instructional style. For all these reasons, we will intentionally build into our practice a wide range of approaches to God and godly living.

We understand each member of every class to be a minister whose purpose in belonging to a class is to be empowered to go out into the world to serve God and humanity. We will trust the active learners among us and see them as servant companions. We will respect the fact that they may at times resist quiet introspection, study, and emotional expressions of faith because a more active approach to God means more to them. We know they will help to keep all of us more honest as stewards of the gospel as good news for the poor, the sick, the lonely, and the vulnerable. We will stretch our religious vocabulary and our understanding of God, honoring and inviting the transcendent God to dwell among us and find in us well-prepared souls, learning from the mystics in our midst. Moreover, we will introduce a wide range of possible prayer forms and approaches to watching over one another in love. This variety will enrich the practice of all the members and respect those members for whom the standard approach to prayer and meditation provided by *This Day: A Wesleyan Way of Prayer* is not consistently satisfying. In these ways we expect to foster a holistic spiritual community.

In summary, the *Class Leader's Manual for Use With* This Day seeks to integrate diverse personalities, as well as a variety of religious practices, into the spiritual life of the *Class Meeting*. In recruiting members, the *Class Leader* will deliberately invite people who might not naturally choose to learn and work together, in order to foster a balanced and holistic practice of faith. Over time, the *Class Leader* will expose the members to the full range of spiritual paths that emerge out of the Christian experience of God. The *Class Leader* will encourage all members to experiment with unfamiliar spiritual disciplines, including: retreating for solitude, image-less meditation, nonpersonal language about God, contemplative prayer, critical thinking, and direct action.

7

Alternative *Forms of Prayer*

Diverse Prayer Forms

A rich diversity of prayer forms and other religious practices has developed over the course of many centuries and out of the practice of a wide range of cultures. These are now available for our use within the context of the Christian faith. We can freely experiment with them and adapt them to our needs and interests. They should be seen as a way of honoring the many age levels, learning styles, and personality types within the *Class Meeting*. Out of respect for diversity and changes in mood, need, or circumstance, the thoughtful *Class Leader* will seek opportunities to introduce these many valid ways of relating to God.

The alternative prayer forms should be understood as supplementary to *This Day: A Wesleyan Way of Prayer*, rather than as substitutes for the standard *daily office*. Care should be taken to demonstrate where and how each of these options might be used within the *daily office*. For example, instead of simply reading the psalm for the day, one might sing it in the form of a hymn or a chant. One might paraphrase a portion of it in a prayer journal or create a breath prayer from a particular set of words or parallel phrases within the psalm. Instead of pondering a biblical reading, pray the passage by writing about it in a prayer journal. Instead of praying the collect of the day every day of the week, one might occasionally prefer to focus on a symbol of the faith or spend time in silence with a name for God. Ultimately, the purpose of introducing a wide range of prayer forms is to help members develop skills and practices that most readily support them in their journey toward God. Doing so will ultimately enhance the effectiveness of the various movements of prayer within the standard *daily office*.

Verbal Prayer

Praying the Name of God

Most people approach God through words, either spoken or read. Simply calling God by name is a form of verbal prayer. Understanding that all language functions as symbol and does not itself contain the object, person, or reality to which it refers, religious people have enjoyed calling God by many names. Jews avoided the revealed name of God, YHWH, by referring to God as "Lord," "Mighty God," "Savior," "Wind," and a host of other names that described some aspect of God or the God-human relationship.

Finding the reference to God that is most comfortable and helpful, and then claiming that name for God as a prayer form, can free worshipers from stumbling over language that obstructs their access to God. For example, some people find Jesus' preferred name for God offensive. Jesus approached God as "Abba" or "Father." One can pray in the name and spirit of Jesus without using his preferred name for God, as long as the name chosen reflects the same trust, submission to divine authority, and love for God that Jesus took to prayer.

Unceasing Prayer

The apostle Paul encouraged his converts to "pray without ceasing" or to "pray continually" (1 Thessalonians 5:17). Christians have found many ways to follow his guidance, while recognizing that no method is in itself sacrosanct. Only as the Holy Spirit inspires prayer within the believer and conforms the mind, heart, and soul to the character of Christ can unceasing prayer be achieved. Still, several tools of faith assist those who seek a constant relationship with God.

One of these *forms of prayer* is the crossculturally significant and single phrase prayer, "Alleluia." It simply means "Praise the Lord." The worshiper may say it once or many times, sing it as a complex refrain, or chant it as a meditation. Some use the words, "I love you, Lord." Others repeat the classic Jesus Prayer, "Lord Jesus Christ, Son of God, have mercy on me, a sinner." (See Brother Lawrence, *The Practice of the Presence of God* [Nashville: Upper Room Devotional Classics]; see also Marjorie J. Thompson, *Soul Feast*, p. 47.) By using such a simple prayer form, the worshiper can allow the phrase to remain in his or her consciousness for long periods of time. In doing so, he or she maintains awareness of the presence of God and enjoys ongoing prayer while engaged in manual work, walking, or resting.

Breath Prayer

Breath prayer, a slightly more complex form of verbal prayer, provides a means by which people initiate a conscious relationship with God. The one praying may begin by selecting a name for God and a single, brief petition that represents the greatest need of one's soul. For example: Inhale the words, "Spirit of God." Exhale the words, "Let me rest in you." The one praying never speaks the words. He or she simply thinks the words in silence, while breathing in and out rhythmically and meditating for several minutes.

This practice is both simple and utterly to the point. It allows the one praying to explore the many nuances of meaning in the few words being used, as well as the implications and validity of the petition. Frequently, supplicants will modify their petition, or move into an alternative name for God, having discovered a more perfect way to express themselves. Almost certainly, the breath prayer leads to a sense of fulfillment, in terms of both communion with God and answered prayer.

An added advantage of this form of verbal prayer is that it can be used with eyes open, while driving or waiting in a line. It can be used quickly and easily in the midst of an explosive or otherwise stressful situation to calm the nerves and gain perspective. Ideally, however, it will be used in the context of the *daily office* as a way of preparing for time with God and with Scripture, or as a time of responding to the Word of God at the close of the *daily office*.

Recitation

Memorized prayer is a time-honored way of learning to pray and of returning to the core of one's faith and values. Recitation of traditional prayers can foster a dynamic interaction between listening and speaking to God. The Lord's Prayer and the Twenty-third Psalm are classic examples of universally significant and easily recited prayers. By praying them aloud at a slow pace, the worshiper can enjoy the cadence of the poetry, meditate on each phrase and image, and allow the formal prayer to guide inner prayerfulness.

These relatively long prayers can be used in a shorter form to inspire breath prayer. For example, one can meditate on the words, "Shepherd/ Lead me" or "My cup/overflows." By using these images from the familiar psalm, the one praying recalls the entire context, without using all the words, and dwells prayerfully in a particularly helpful part of the prayer.

Similar use can be made of the Lord's Prayer by breathing the words, "Thy kingdom come/ On earth as in heaven." By meditating on these phrases, one recalls the full weight of meaning that Jesus took to his message, its proclamation, and its realization. In this way, the worshiper brings the inner and outer self into harmony with God and approaches life out of the vision and hope of Jesus.

The Daily Office

The *daily office,* or order of prayer for morning and evening prayer, provides a still more complex form of verbal prayer. It begins with the prayer of the day or "collect" to be said by all the people. These traditional prayers, written in contemporary language in *This Day: A Wesleyan Way of Prayer,* reflect a wide range of occasions and needs, spiritual goals, and postures of the soul. By using standard prayer forms over the course of each month, the disciple avoids spiritual stagnation or repetitive use of the most convenient approach to prayers for self, church, others, and more global concerns. Those who use the *daily office* accept and respect the spiritual guidance of the Church that valued these prayers and preserved them for use today.

The *daily office* can become a sensory and kinetic prayer form, as well as a mindful or cognitive approach to God. By saying the prayers aloud, singing the canticles, and changing one's posture from kneeling to standing to prostrating one's self before God, the *daily office* can engage the whole person and become an active expression of love for God. Note that the *daily office* can be said and sung within the *Class Meeting,* as well as in private or with a larger group.

Sung Prayer

Hymns, songs, and spiritual songs or choruses provide a still more dynamic form of verbal prayer. Prayers set to music and sung can provide focus and participation, especially for sensory, kinetic, and affective learners who benefit from engaging their bodies and emotions, as well as their minds, in worship. The poetry and sounds of sung prayer can help the worshiper transcend the limitations of a rational approach to God by giving expression to feelings that otherwise may have remained unexplored. The Kyrie Eleison, the Gloria Patri, the Gloria in excelsis, the Doxology, the Nunc Dimittis (Luke 2:29-32), the Sanctus, and the Canticle of Mary or Magnificat (Luke 1:46-55) are among the sung prayers found within the standard *daily office* of the *Book of Common Prayer.* Myriad contemporary choruses offer postmodern disciples ample resources for sung prayer that may be occasionally substituted for the collect, psalm, or other ascription of praise or canticle.

The Psalter

The Book of Psalms provides a readily available and classic prayer book for people of any age level or life circumstance. One can benefit from praying some psalms every day for a week, finding fresh meaning in each reading. On the other hand, many psalms express sentiments contrary to the spirit and teachings of Jesus. These remnants of an earlier understanding of God can be impediments to prayer, rather than bridges over which the soul passes easily into the Divine Presence. For this reason, most prayer books and lectionaries recommend using the psalms selectively.

This Day: A Wesleyan Way of Prayer suggests, however, that class members use all of the psalms as guides to prayer. The Book of Psalms, in all its diversity, strength, and weakness, provides a means of expressing the whole range of human emotions, both conscious and preconscious. By using all of the psalms, we meet expressions of fear, pride, doubt, anger, contrition, grief, gratitude, trust, and hope; and, in so doing, find validation for the many moods of our own faith journey.

By allowing the psalmists to speak for us in prayer, we learn to deplore the worst traits of human nature, live gently with our oftentimes myopic faith, and grow through times of anguish toward trust in God. Ultimately, faithful use of the Book of Psalms will reveal some of the greatest treasures of devotional literature. The wise believer will underline or otherwise mark the treasures hidden among the many pages of thanksgiving, confession, petition, supplication, intercession, lament, and praise.

Traditional and Extemporaneous Prayer

John Wesley probably used the "Office for Morning and Evening Prayer" found in the *Book of Common Prayer*, on a daily basis. He read it aloud in the privacy of his home and was known to call his household to join him early in the morning. The *Book of Common Prayer* was widely distributed and a staple of British household furnishings. The written prayers of the Anglican Church, therefore, provided the standard format for private and family prayer among early Methodists in England and Ireland.

At the same time, however, Wesley used extemporaneous prayer in his private devotions one or two days a week and encouraged his followers to do so. He preferred to pray extemporaneously in the class and *band* meetings. Following his example, early Methodists learned to rely on the inner guidance of the Spirit in prayer.

Some Methodists, however, have never learned to pray extemporaneously. Many feel they do not know how to pray at all. People feel more or less awkward doing so in front of others and may appreciate written prayers to guide them in praying for themselves, others, the church, and the world.

When introducing extemporaneous prayer, as *Class Leader* you should avoid going around the circle, expecting each one to lead in turn. Instead, take time to explain what a sentence petition is and how and why people pray spontaneously. Establish an atmosphere in which simplicity of speech, inspired by compassion and faith, become the norm. Follow a specific procedure and use it regularly. This will allow your class to move gracefully from the *reflection* into Spirit-led prayer, without the awkwardness of instruction.

Begin by saying that you will open and close the time of prayer. Tell the class in advance that you will allow time for any member to express, in a simple sentence or phrase, anything they wish to take to God in prayer. Urge members to spend a moment in silence after each member speaks before offering another prayer. This will help to focus the faith of the entire class on each petition and encourage listening for the guidance of the Spirit in leading the next petition. Ask everyone to bear one another's burdens and articulate prayer in response to the needs that have been expressed within the group. As *Class Leader*, you may need to broaden the scope of prayer, over the course of a month of *Class Meetings*, to include the church, the community, and the world.

Model brevity in your own initial sentence prayer. For example, you might say, "Lord, we come into your presence with open hearts and minds. Guide us as we pray." Wait in silence until all who wish to speak have expressed themselves. Then say, "And now with the confidence of the children of God, let us pray: 'Our Father, who art in heaven ...'"

Occasionally invite class members to lead the opening *Prayer for Illumination* or the closing blessing modeled after standard prayers, but expressed in their own words. You will need to model spiritual discernment by calling for prayer at times of special need, confusion, tension, or other distress, either in the life of the group or in an individual's life. For example, if someone reports that they have just come from learning that a parent has a terminal illness, you will want to lead the class into extemporaneous intercessory prayer. Over time and with practice, the class will develop the confidence to pray spontaneously without relying either on you as *Class Leader* or on prepared prayers. This will enrich their private and family prayer life. Nevertheless, the standard resources of traditional prayer should provide the regular daily nourishment for a vital relationship with God and inform the opening and closing prayers of the *Class Meeting*.

Journaling

Keeping a prayer journal can be a powerful form of verbal prayer. It can be used for the purpose of recording what God is saying through the Scriptures in the context of daily prayer. Journaling as a form of extemporaneous prayer encourages us to allow the Spirit to search us, know us, and pray through us as we write. In essence, it can be used as a way of exploring one's soul in the presence of God or engaging in prayer for others.

When we express what has been haunting us, either through conversation or in writing, we do something that biblical people would have called "naming the demon." By identifying the concern in writing, we address it directly. The act of writing down on a piece of paper something that has been a vague matter of intuition and feeling up to that point empowers the soul both to look objectively at the matter and to present it before God. Put another way, through prayer journaling, we expose what has been imposing itself on us at a subconscious or preconscious level. We objectify the problem and can then treat it as a reality separate from our inmost self. The following instructions can be used when you as a *Class Leader* seek to teach journaling.

- Begin with a clean page, preferably in a bound notebook. You may or may not want to date the entry. This writing is for your use alone.

- Address your journal entry to God, using your favorite name for God, as in a letter addressed to the Source, Guide, and Goal of your life.

- Pause to be with God in stillness and reverence. Then offer yourself to God as you are. Open your soul, mind, and emotions to God.

- Freely express yourself in God's presence, following the stream of consciousness as it emerges, pausing frequently to listen and reflect in the light of God's company.

- Allow God to speak to you through the act of writing, as if you were engaged in dialogue with God. Continue until all that must be said has been recorded.

- Close with praise and thanksgiving, followed by an Amen.

Another dialogical approach to prayerful journaling has been suggested by Marjorie Thompson in her book *Soul Feast* (p. 43).

- Compose a conversation with a personality from scripture. You might choose the story of Jesus healing the woman with the issue of blood or imagine yourself present as Jesus heals the man brought to him on the cot that his friends lower through the roof of Peter's home in Capernaum.

- After reading the Scripture, you may identify with the one to whom Jesus ministers and seek to embody that character as you write.

- Place yourself in the story. Feel the events as they unfold.

- Record your experience in the format of a dramatic dialogue.

- Note any questions that surface, and any personal needs you might like to take to Jesus.

- Pause to receive the response you need from the Lord, whose presence transcends space and time. Record what you hear.

In Summary

Verbal prayer forms are both the easiest way to approach God and the most common. Those who prefer to approach God through reason rely heavily on spoken prayer. Written and spoken prayer work well for most learning styles and personality types, especially when ample opportunity is given to utilize breath prayer, journaling, poetry, and sung prayer.

Traditional prayer forms echo biblical language, spiritual values, and images of God. People who prefer to approach God through mystical awareness or intuitive intelligence may, however, find the language of most traditional prayer less than helpful. These class members need to experiment until they find a few verbal prayer forms which work well for them. At times they will need to remain silent while others speak. It is they who will lead others beyond talking to God toward listening for God and hearing one another's unspoken, yet soulful cries.

Silent Prayer

For purposes of offering alternatives to verbal approaches to prayer, it is well to exclude written prayers from the category of silent prayer forms. We focus here instead on what has traditionally been called "contemplation." The goal of contemplation is to spend time being with God, aware of God's indwelling presence, and enjoying the stillness of shared eternity.

Contemplative prayer is one of the most difficult *forms of prayer* to sustain. Most people must practice this form of meditation regularly over many months before they are able to employ it with ease. Others who are introspective, mystical, and intuitive by nature will find this form of prayer natural and deeply gratifying. It can be entered into with the assistance of either a verbal or a visual image, or with eyes closed and the mind still.

Imageless Silence

Apophatic prayer is silent prayer without the aid of either verbal or visual images. It can be understood as sensory asceticism or self-denial. It is a way of emptying one's self in order to be filled with God. It relies exclusively on the Holy Spirit's communing with the human spirit. Paul describes this form of prayer in Romans 8:26-27:

> Likewise the Spirit helps us in our weakness; for we do not know how to pray as we ought, but that very Spirit intercedes with sighs too deep for words. And God, who searches the heart, knows what is the mind of the Spirit, because the Spirit intercedes for the saints according to the will of God. (See also Philippians 2:6-7.)

Sacred silence often emerges only after one exhausts other means of prayer. It comes when we are ready to cast ourselves on God alone. For example, one might begin with the usual *daily office*, including the reading of Scripture and prayers for self, others, and the church, and then pause during a time of silent reflection to pray the breath prayer taken from John 17:21b: Inhale, "I in Thee"; exhale: "Thou in me." Pray this prayer for some time until you fall silent and find rest in God.

John Wesley valued silence as the highest form of prayer. In describing the unceasing prayer of a Methodist, he wrote: "Nor is he always crying aloud to God, or calling upon him in words.... But at all times the language of his heart is this: 'Thou brightness of eternal glory, unto thee is my heart, though without a voice, and my silence speaketh unto thee.' And this is true prayer and this alone" (*The Character of a Methodist,* found in Welch, p. 297).

Visual Silence

Cataphatic prayer traditionally employs a visual focus as a means of communion with God. For example, one may fix one's attention on a simple cross, a communion goblet, a flame, or a water jar. The external object signifies meaning derived from a biblical source. Icons serve this purpose for Eastern Orthodox Christians. By way of meditating on the symbol and its meaning, the worshiper sees beyond the work of art to the God who is always nearer than the breath in our mouths.

Ideally, the contemplative person transcends himself or herself and becomes one with God and one with the universe. God reigns and the ego is dethroned. The fruits of silence before God include compassion, reverence for life, and humility.

This same experience can be gained without an external visual focus. With one's eyes closed, one can visualize the glory of God as light that shines in the darkness and thereby enter into sacred mystery. This form of meditation is most accessible to mystics and others who have previously received visions. Visual learners, particularly those who have successfully participated in guided meditations, can recall previous moments of visual epiphany and reenter those experiences by meditating on them.

The most gratifying and transformational experiences of prayer come not as a result of disciplined practice but as a free gift from God, surprising the recipients and calling them into life in the Spirit. Paul described this experience when writing to the church at Corinth:

> When one turns to the Lord, the veil is removed. Now the Lord is the Spirit, and where the Spirit of the Lord is, there is freedom. And all of us, with unveiled faces, seeing the glory of the Lord as though reflected in a mirror, are being transformed into the same image from one degree of glory to another; for this comes from the Lord, the Spirit.... For it is the God who said, 'Let light shine out of darkness,' who has shone in our hearts to give the light of the knowledge of the glory of God in the face of Jesus Christ." (2 Corinthians 3:16-18–4:6)

Others testify to the foretaste of eternal life or the inner witness of God's Spirit with our spirit that we are children of God (refer to Romans 8:15-16). Paul described a peace that passes all understanding (Philippians 4:7). John Wesley called the experience "assurance."

Re-membering Prayer

Re-membering prayer is an essentially nonverbal form of meditation aimed at restoring wholeness. It can be especially helpful for members who find it difficult to concentrate in prayer or are enduring a particularly stressful life passage. The practice acknowledges the experience and the complex interplay of conscious, subconscious, and preconscious interaction of sensation, emotion, thought, and soulful longing for life. The many aspects of the self, including the physical body, the psyche or emotional self, and the mind or rational self, often compete for attention. They distract the inmost self from its work.

When the soul is free to commune with God, then the whole person experiences enhanced well-being. The goal of re-membering is to bring the many dimensions of the self into submission to the Spirit, so that they no longer distract the soul from communion with God. The self remembers its source and functions harmoniously.

The usual practice of re-membering begins with relaxing the body. Flexing and tensing muscles, regulating breathing, and assuming a posture of meditation typically provide the starting place for this form of prayer. An alternative is "sauntering," walking gently on the earth as an act of affirming life and being present to the moment. Vigorous exercise, such as calisthenics or aerobics, can help release tension and overcome anxiety.

The next phase of re-membering addresses the psyche. It involves naming and releasing feelings into God's presence until the emotions no longer control one's attention in prayer. This stage of meditation may evoke tears, sighs, or song, depending upon the depth and variety of emotions being experienced. The goal is to unpack feelings that may not have been recognized, experience them fully, and then release them to God as an act of faith.

Beyond the release of one's feelings to God comes the release of one's thoughts. These may include concerns for self, others, the church, and the world, as well as questions or doubts. One may surrender these concerns as petitions or through intercessory prayer. The mental work of re-membering may include thanksgiving, confession, and supplication. Tame distracting thoughts by recording any unfinished business that surfaces in the midst of prayer in a journal.

Ultimately, re-membering leads toward stillness. Having worked through the earlier phases, the self is now empty, clean, and available to receive God. Sanctity has been restored to the temple of God's Spirit. In the silence of one's inner self, one may perceive God within. Quiet rest and active listening for God will follow. This form of prayer can provide the necessary preparation for hearing God's Word through Scripture.

Practice re-membering prayer at least once a week, before reading the appointed lectionary text. Doing so will deepen the level of satisfaction and enhance the formative power of living with God's Word. This form of nonverbal prayer will require an additional ten minutes in devotional time. If one chooses to saunter or engage in vigorous exercise in the care of the body, thirty minutes for re-membering prayer is needed.

Lectio Divina (Holy Reading)

Listening for the Word of God through Scripture and other inspired writing, such as hymns and inspirational classics, can be among the most creative and transformational *forms of prayer*. The ancient Hebrews knew that when God speaks and humanity responds by faith, salvation unfolds. God's Word is creative. (See Genesis 1:3; Isaiah 55:11; Romans 1:16.)

Lectio divina is a patterned approach to hearing from God, guided either by a lectionary of daily readings or by a sequential reading of one or more books of the Bible. In either case, the one praying the Scripture reads the appointed passage for familiarity, reviews it for understanding, and revisits it a third time in order to listen for the Word of God as God may be speaking to the reader. *Lecto divina* concludes with silence and commitment to act upon God's Word (James 1:23).

John Wesley advised his followers:

> First: Assign some stated time every day for this employment; and observe it, so far as you possibly can, inviolably. But if necessary business, which you could not foresee or defer, should sometimes rob you of your hour of retirement, take the next to it; or, if you cannot have that, at least the nearest you can. Secondly: Prepare yourself for reading, by purity of intention singly aiming at the good of your soul, and by fervent prayer to see God's will, and give you a firm resolution to perform it.... Thirdly: Be sure to read, not cursorily or hastily, but leisurely, seriously, and with great attention; with proper pauses and intervals, and that you may allow time for the enlightening of the divine grace. To this end, recollect, every now and then, what you have read, and consider how to reduce it to practice. (Rueben Job, *Guide to Prayer for All God's People*, p. 119)

When reading the psalms, for example, the disciple may read through three psalms before being moved by a particular passage. Having found this gem, like treasure unearthed in a field, the reader prizes, marks, and enjoys it. Those who keep a journal will want to record the passage.

Class Leaders who are facilitating a study of a book of the Bible or of the lectionary, as in using the *International Lesson Series,* can ask class members to read the scriptural material in advance during their daily prayer time as *lectio divina*. This will encourage approaching the biblical material as a means of listening for the Word of God, rather than as a merely academic exercise. To facilitate this, the *Class Leader* might suggest adding prayerful reading of the Bible passages contained in the study to the daily readings in *This Day: A Wesleyan Way of Prayer.*

A similar approach to holy reading uses hymns for *lectio divina.* Bishop Rueben Job in his *Guide to Prayer for All God's People* (Nashville: Upper Room Books, 1990) suggests praying the words of a particular hymn every day throughout a given week. In so doing, the worshiper rediscovers the hymn as sacred poetry and often finds a particular phrase or verse freshly meaningful. Some members will choose to commit a phrase or verse of the hymn to memory and sing it throughout the day.

Active Prayer

When the body is seen not as an obstacle to communion with God but as a means of access, the sensory learner discovers his or her giftedness for prayer. To walk on the earth as on holy ground, for example, breathing deeply of fresh air and absorbing sunlight through the skin can be a way of praying, when it is done as a conscious act of holy living. It can enhance awareness of the privilege of being alive and encourage fuller participation in eternal life within the present moment.

To touch someone lovingly and respectfully can be a profound form of nonverbal prayer. After the breaking of bread and the prayers, early Christians offered one another a holy kiss (Romans 16:16; 1 Corinthians 16:20; 2 Corinthians 13:12; 1 Thessalonians 5:26; 1 Peter 5:14). The laying on of hands, commonly practiced by Jesus as a component of healing ministry, still conveys the power of faith when practiced by those who understand its place and offer their hands in divine service.

Bodily movement can engage the senses in kinetic worship. Dancing can be a way of expressing faith. Lifting hands in praise or prostrating one's self, crossing one's self, or otherwise using one's body to worship God can be a helpful ritual. When one stands erect with arms outstretched, for example, the body takes the form of the cross and the soul feels itself crucified with Christ. When the worshiper takes a fetal position, with head on the ground, the soul feels its dependency upon God and the ego sees itself in light of the vastness of the universe, history, humanity, and the divine. When one stands with legs together and arms reaching upward, allowing the body to take the form of a communion goblet, the soul assumes a posture of receptivity to the Spirit of God. By sitting quietly with palms open, resting on the lap, one expresses readiness to partake of the daily bread that proceeds from God. Simply kneeling before an altar can bring the faithful into an encounter with God, as can taking off one's shoes while standing in silence before God.

Tactile spiritual exercises can be equally significant as approaches to God. When one holds a mustard seed between two fingers and remembers Jesus' parable, new dimensions of faith can germinate within the soul. Consider the value of thoughtfully drinking a glass of water while recalling the words of Jesus, "Out of the believer's heart shall flow rivers of living water" (John 7:38). Choose a favorite vase as a symbol of one's inmost self and then place it on a private altar or on the windowsill above the kitchen sink as a visual reminder to serve as a vessel of God's Spirit (1 Corinthians 6:19-20). One man wears sandals as a reminder of his vocation as a follower of Jesus.

Simple rituals can sanctify time and bring a sense of holy order to life. Many people light a candle during prayer. Some place a stone or other significant object at a place of prayer to mark it as sacred space, following the example of Jacob and other ancients (Genesis 35:9-15). Holding the Bible in silence, while sitting quietly, can be a form of sensory communion. These acts can lead toward a profound awareness of God's presence and of resting in God.

A carpenter friend once told me that helping to build a house for someone else is a spiritually grounding experience. Hammering a nail, changing a tire, sawing wood, or cleaning an upper shelf for someone who could not do it alone can be a way of connecting with Christ—by serving another. Remember Jesus touching the leper, laying hands on the crippled, or washing the feet of his disciples. The sensory learner may pray best while actively caring for the earth or for another human being.

Auditory Prayer

Many people learn best through hearing. They experience reality, including God, through speaking and being spoken to, as well as through other sounds. For example, a loud gong or the ringing of a bell can serve as a call to prayer that resonates deep within the soul. Once, while visiting a Greek monastery, I heard the sounding of a chime and felt moved beyond words to enter not only sacred space, but an inner place of awareness. Canting or chanting inspires meditation, even when the words are sung in a language strange to the hearer, such as Latin, Greek, French, Arabic, or Hebrew. Recently, while I was visiting Bethlehem, a Syrian Orthodox Christian recited the Lord's Prayer in Aramaic. The sounds of Jesus' native language, coupled with the experience of the place and the meaning of this universal prayer, invited me into a holy awareness. Even a chorus of birdsong or of peepers can lead to exultation or to a sense of oneness with life in all its forms.

Many find the sounds of running water a way of remembering their baptism and being thankful. Millions of people from all faith traditions find watching and hearing the sounds of waves crashing against the shoreline or rippling along a sandy beach a soothing, cleansing guide to resting the soul in God. Attending to these sounds in the context of Christian meaning allows the unconscious self to flow freely in harmony with the God whose cleansing Spirit bathes and satisfies the soul. Meditating in this way refreshes and restores body, mind, and spirit. The psalmist suggested this experience when he wrote, "The LORD is my shepherd, I shall not want.... he leads me beside still waters; he restores my soul" (Psalm 23:1, 2b-3a).

Guided Meditation

In the context of a class session or retreat, the quiet and resonant voice of the leader can guide the auditory, intuitive, or affective learner into restful listening and being with God. Even those who prefer to approach God through reason or action can sometimes be engaged in this type of exercise for a short period of time. Help the group to view the imagination as a sacred tool for approaching God.

Scripture provides abundant source material for guided meditation. By using biblical narratives and prayer-poems, this interfaith form of prayer becomes explicitly Christian. Those who may feel uncomfortable with it at first will find it easy and natural to begin, for example, with Psalm 23 or Psalm 121.

Introduce guided meditation by affirming that the Scriptures use story and metaphor to help the faithful know God. Invite the group to use their imaginations in order to experience the scriptural meditation they are about to take. Ask them to follow the leader's voice. Assure them that they will be guided both with words and through silence, during which everyone will have the opportunity to pause in the places where the images of the psalm take them. Ask participants to sit upright in a comfortable position, with palms open and resting on their laps.

Begin by reciting the psalm or other scriptural passage phrase by phrase, pausing between each image to encourage the group to spend time, for example, by still waters, lying on the green grass, seated at the Lord's table, feeling the anointing with oil, and dwelling in the house of the Lord. Before saying the Amen at the close of the psalm, encourage the class to sit in silence, reflecting on their experience and observing any singularly precious element of the meditation. Finally, encourage everyone to return mentally and emotionally to the room where they are seated and to open their eyes when they are ready to do so. Say the Amen after a few moments of waiting in silence.

It can be very enriching to supplement a guided meditation with a visual or sensory focus. Recently, I led a group in a meditation with the story of the woman who anointed Jesus' body for burial (Mark 14:3-9). After the Amen, I offered a vial of spikenard to the group and suggested that they might like to anoint the person next to them, as a way of honoring the Spirit of Christ in one another. The scent of perfume and of prayer filled the room.

In guiding a group with Psalm 23, the obvious gift to make is that of oil. Olive oil works best. Invite all who desire to be anointed to stand for prayer or to take their turn being seated in a central chair. Both laity and clergy can perform this anointing in Jesus' name. As with the perfume, the members may anoint one another.

The resources for guided meditation are as vast as the scope of biblical narrative and poetry and as limited as the boundaries of faithful imagination. The gift that the *Class Leader* makes in guiding a group of believers into communion with God through guided meditation is beyond words and entirely worth the time it will take away from study or a more traditional *reflection*. Once a group has experienced guided meditation, members may be able to meditate with Scripture on their own, allowing the written Word to speak more readily to their emotions, will, and inmost self. The witness of faith that often results from such an experience reflects the state of the participants' souls and can replace the *reflection*. It will naturally lead into group prayer, either silent or spoken.

Guided meditation and visualization inspired by Scripture can also empower intercessory prayer. By prayerfully taking another to Jesus for healing, for example, we can hear from God on behalf of the person for whom we pray. We can receive the gift of faith by which to encourage the faith and wholeness of a friend or family member.

Relational Prayer

Christian Conferencing

Believers can learn to pray while conversing around spiritual and moral concerns. John Wesley required his preachers "to converse seriously, usefully, and closely." He held them accountable for praying before doing so, approaching every conversation with a "determinate end" (Minutes, 1747 in "Conference as a Means of Grace," *Early American Methodism*, Russell E. Richey, Indiana University Press, p. 74). This can be encouraged by way of a call to *Prayer for Illumination* before the conversation begins and by way of a prayer for discernment whenever confusion or disagreement surfaces. Enhance *Christian Conferencing* by observing a time of silence after each person speaks. In this way, the conversation becomes a deliberate practice of seeking the "mind of Christ" (1 Corinthians 2:15-16).

The response of the class to a member's confession during the *reflection* should be a form of relational prayer. Otherwise, group response can be a superficial I'm-O.K.-you're-O.K. chatter or a pedantic exhortation in which members impose their experience on one another. Without an atmosphere of prayer, active listening can become uninvited advice. When the class pauses in silence to listen deeply and respond as they are inspired by the Spirit, on the other hand, all may hear from God and be transformed (1 Corinthians 12:4-11; 14:1, 3).

Celebrating Together

The apostle Paul advises the church, "Rejoice always, pray without ceasing, give thanks in all circumstances; for this is the will of God in Christ Jesus for you. Do not quench the Spirit" (1 Thessalonians 5:16-19). When breakthroughs occur or healing takes place, when souls find refreshment in God, or when redemption takes place, the people of God must express their joy. Praise and thanksgiving become more than liturgical acts. They can become holy moments of corporate worship. Acts of celebration may occur spontaneously in the midst of the *reflection* or during study, in the gathering time before class or in the hallway afterward. Celebration may take the form of a hug or tears, an exchange of Scripture or prayer, or an offer of personal friendship.

Often such a witness of redeeming *grace* requires storytelling. The role of the *Class Leader* is to facilitate and guide this form of relational prayer when it occurs within the *Class Meeting*. One of the great challenges of guiding a class is knowing when to redirect persons who may so enjoy telling their stories that the class will never get to the stated business of the meeting. Modeling is one of the more effective ways of leading. *Class Leaders* who celebrate briefly and concisely set a pattern for others.

John Wesley provided for celebrating the *grace* of God outside of the *Class Meeting* in three specific ways. First, he required all Methodists to partake of the Eucharist whenever it was offered and at least weekly on the Lord's Day. The Eucharist interprets all praise and thanksgiving in light of the life, death, and resurrection of Jesus. The liturgy invites communicants to celebrate the steadfast love of God and the mercy and strength available through Jesus.

Second, Wesley called the classes together to meet as Methodist societies. The *society* meetings occurred on a weekday evening and were dedicated to prayer, singing, preaching, and testimonies to God's saving *grace*. Class members knew that they would have opportunity to bear witness to their faith in these extended sessions.

Third, Wesley adapted the Moravian Love Feast to the needs of the Methodists. Particularly in North American Methodism, quarterly Love Feasts featured testimonies and led to revival, fondly called "a melting time" in many early Methodist journals (see "Community, Fraternity, and Order" in Richey, p. 3). A guide for the contemporary *Love Feast* can be found in *This Day: A Wesleyan Way of Prayer*. The *Class Leader* will be wise to offer a variety of opportunities during which class members can anticipate the privilege and responsibility of bearing witness to their faith publicly.

Since most one-hour *Class Meetings* will not provide adequate time for a full expression of the *grace* of God in the lives of the members, it is well that we restore the old tradition of quarterly Love Feasts as a feature of twenty-first century Methodism. The early pattern provided for the Love Feast before Sunday morning worship. Regular retreats need to be planned that conclude with the Lord's Supper. An annual renewal weekend provides for celebrating the fruits of the *Class Meeting* system. During these public occasions, class members will rejoice in the Lord and encourage others with their testimonies to God's *grace*.

Interactive Prayer

A number of prayer forms can be integrated into *Class Meeting* experiences, including the study portion of class time. One useful verbal prayer form is dialogical prayer, in which two people consciously relate to God while speaking with each other. This can be particularly helpful in conflict resolution or as a substitute for secular debate, when a group is studying two equally valid but opposing points of view on a critical issue.

Role play can be another form of active, spoken prayer. Recently a member revealed that she needed to forgive her father who is no longer alive. After having heard her story, I assumed the role of her dad. She spoke from the perspective both of herself as she was when a particularly hurtful incident occurred and as the woman she now is. This prayerful form of role play enabled profound healing.

A similar and equally powerful application of interactive prayer, useful in the midst of Bible study, engages class members in impersonating characters within a passage of Scripture. Class members are assigned different roles. Other members are onlookers. The passage is read aloud to familiarize participants with their characters and with the dynamics of the story. The passage is read a second time so that everyone can place themselves in the midst of the biblical events. The class is given time to digest their experiences. Onlookers share what they saw and heard. As an alternative, class members are asked to maintain their roles and talk to one another about what they have witnessed, sharing the impact that these experiences had on them. The activity is closed with silence and a brief prayer of thanksgiving and commitment. The use of role play in lectionary studies brings the Scripture to life. It creates a "Word event" in which God speaks afresh to those who place themselves in the midst of biblical epiphanies (Gerhard Ebeling).

Incorporating Alternative Prayer Forms Within the *Class Meeting*

Having become more aware of the diverse needs and opportunities for Christian prayer, as a *Class Leader* you will search for and create settings in which these prayer forms can be learned and used. Encourage all members to discover their preferred learning style and to experiment with the prayer forms best suited to their needs. Suggest that each class member choose one alternative prayer form and practice it for at least four consecutive weeks, until it either proves less than satisfactory or becomes an integral means of unceasing prayer.

Several suggestions follow:

1. When meeting with the class for the first time to orient members to the method of the *Class Meeting* system and develop a group

covenant, introduce *This Day: A Wesleyan Way of Prayer.* Indicate that, over the course of time, you will introduce a wide variety of prayer forms. This will reassure members who do not readily find access to God through liturgical prayers. Introduce relational prayer immediately, seeking the form of praying together that best suits the needs and tastes of your membership.

2. Within the first six weeks of using the prayer book, begin using one of the alternative prayer forms, either at the beginning or at the close of each class session.

3. Plan a retreat weekend for all of the *Class Meetings* in the church during which the various alternative *forms of prayer* can be experienced. Use the *daily office* in the morning, at midday, and in the evening, taking care to demonstrate how various types of prayer enhance the standard elements of the *daily office.*

Conclusions

In order to maintain interest and foster discipleship in adults of all ages, you as the *Class Leader* must choose prayer forms appropriate to the needs of your class members. Young adults typically prefer structured prayer that is contemporary in style, including responsorial prayer or a call and response format. They often respond well to multisensory worship. For this reason, every effort should be made to provide visual, tactile, auditory, dialogical, or dramatic and kinetic prayer forms in *Class Meetings* that are designed to meet their needs. Like everyone else, however, young adults need safe spiritual community in which they can reveal themselves and be understood in the context of *Christian Conferencing.* Many enjoy journaling.

Young and middle adults typically lead highly active lives. They need tools for quieting themselves and resting in God. For this reason, even though they may resist learning to use contemplative *forms of prayer,* you would be wise to expose young and middle-aged adults to breath prayer and *lectio divina,* as well as to more relational and sensory/motor prayer forms.

Middle-aged adults and older adults typically benefit more readily than younger adults from solitude, silence, introspective retreating, and guided meditation. They are more likely than their younger counterparts to be able to practice contemplation. In addition, you may find ritual to be freshly meaningful to them.

Older adults benefit from traditional prayers, familiar hymns, and faith-sharing, as well as *lectio divina.* They may find little satisfaction in the kinetic, visual, or tactile forms of meditation. Ultimately, you will seek to foster tolerance in the midst of diversity and a sense of security in experimenting with a wide range of approaches to God.

8

Recognizing Changing Needs Over the Adult Life Span

If we define an adult as anyone over the age of twenty-one and we hope to engage adults of all age levels in a vital discipleship system, then we must prepare to deal with individuals in at least four major life stages. At each of these stages, different tasks must be accomplished in the process of spiritual formation. When the work of one stage of spiritual formation is successfully completed, the adult may move with minimal difficulty through the transition to the next life stage and complete the major tasks of the next stage with relative ease. Inadequate work in the past, however, will handicap the person attempting to move forward into new challenges. Most people have work to redo from an earlier life stage. By identifying the faith formation tasks that need remedial work or reinforcement among the members, you as *Class Leader* serve as a helpful group facilitator and spiritual guide. With a clear sense of the needs of the people you serve, you will be less vulnerable to resistance and less inclined to take the challenges of group members personally.

Suppose that in your class you have an unmarried Caucasian woman just graduating from college, a married Korean American mother who stays at home with two toddlers, a single Caucasian male in his midforties with teenage children, a married African American woman in her fifties, a recently married Hispanic man in his early seventies, and three Caucasian widows in their late seventies, one of whom comes from a Pentecostal church and another who has recently converted from Roman Catholicism. Your class is not yet full, but the diversity of age levels alone represents a fascinating challenge. When you add to this the full range of personality profiles, learning styles, and cultural and racial backgrounds, it becomes clear that the curriculum and prescribed prayers will serve only as the starting place for a dynamic process of building spiritual community. Further complicating the equation is the reality that a great many adults function as if their spiritual development were arrested in early adolescence. They function haltingly with a theology more appropriate for a younger person.

You will need to accept and work with people who have not yet developed age-appropriate faith. For example, a young adult member may be having first-time exposure to Christianity within the *Class Meeting*. This newcomer must learn the basics of the tradition at an elementary level before participating as a peer with other class members. The soul-searching questions of the other members, some of whom may be seeking to develop a personal faith that demythologizes religion, may be confusing and disturbing to a person who is having to make up for years of spiritual formation that others have undertaken at earlier life stages. You will need to determine how best to care for such members, while simultaneously preserving the benefits of the *Class Meeting* for the others.

Many churches find that dividing adults into age-level groupings simplifies this challenge. Still others form classes for "beginners," "seekers," and "disciples." These designations indicate differing levels of work parallel to academic designations such as introductory, intermediate, and advanced. The early *Class Meeting* system of Methodism similarly organized *Class Meetings* for new converts, select *bands* for women and men who were "going on to perfection," and separate *bands* for penitent sinners. This approach may, however, limit crossfertilization and the sharing of wisdom. Moreover, the practical difficulty of providing sufficient membership and leadership for such specialized groupings in a small church makes this approach impractical for most congregations.

You will need to work toward becoming sufficiently competent as a *Class Leader* so as to be able to care for a class diverse in age and stage of faith development. Otherwise, it may be better to offer classes for various levels of readiness. Less experienced *Class Leaders* will be more successful working with relatively homogneous groups of adults.

Young Adults (Ages 21-40)

Young adults are exploring the fit of their inherited faith and developing their own belief system. They need to take control of their worldview and discover their own path to God. They often have many searching questions about the beliefs passed down to them in childhood and early adolescence. They need to translate their concepts of God and Christianity into terms that relate to their new status and perspective as responsible adults. If they are actively searching for adult faith and looking for meaning in life, they will respond well to a faith community where they feel safe asking challenging questions. They will appreciate a thoughtful, open exchange of ideas in the context of mutual respect.

The goal of faith in this life stage is to foster intimacy with self, others, and God, and thereby overcome isolation and doubt. The spiritual life well lived in young adulthood will provide for a sense of inner communion with God and outer communion with the church. Effectively accomplishing the work of young adult faith will allow the believer to discover and develop his or her sense of calling and vocation as a person of God, to apply newly acquired skills to the work of God in the world, and to begin to contribute creatively to the spiritual formation of others. This is what developmental theorists refer to as the "individuative/reflective" stage of faith formation (see James Fowler).

Middle Adults (Ages 40-55)

The middle-aged adult may be dealing for the first time with his or her subconscious. In this process of ego integration, moral concerns become more complex. The polarities of the self become apparent. Middle-aged adults recognize their dark side, or shadow self, and must address it directly through the lens of faith.

The previously extroverted and task-oriented individual becomes more reflective and introspective. The quiet follower may blossom and contribute out of a wealth of creativity that had been submerged under the weight of the multiple tasks of younger adult life. Previously reserved and highly rational people relax and are willing to play again, using their imaginations to explore the nuances and depths of Scripture, prayer, meditation, and resting in God. They are more comfortable with themselves and, therefore, more comfortable with people of differing faith experiences and traditions. Their ability to empathize and keep company with others grows.

Communities of middle-aged adults often help one another rediscover the mystery of faith and their own spiritual nature. Sacred ritual, story, and symbolism take on fresh significance for them. While never abandoning the image of God revealed in Jesus of Nazareth, these adults may gravitate toward a primary experience of God as Spirit. Some of these disciples may seem more like "seekers" than traditional Christians. They are engaged in developing what theorists call "conjunctive faith" (James Fowler).

They require a faith experience that facilitates self-transcendence. Their primary task is to bear fruit and experience fruitfulness, that is, to become generative adult Christians who nurture the faith of others and serve out of their accumulated wisdom and skill (John 15:16).

Older Adults (Ages 55-70)

Empty nesters and young retirees frequently have energy and time for servant ministries that younger adults may not have. They bring to the work of faith formation the desire to remain productive, to preserve a clear sense of purpose and meaning in life, and to simplify their lives. They typically have less tolerance for stress and less stamina than they once enjoyed. Travel and extended family may distract them from consistent participation in leadership roles and Wesleyan *Class Meetings*.

Their primary task, as they continue to grow spiritually, is to develop godly wisdom. Their appropriate and highest goal is to become Christlike. Their chief contribution to the life of the church will be to offer younger believers an example of mature faith.

While many older adults function with a worldview and religious vocabulary typical of an earlier stage of faith formation, they may have a heightened awareness of God-with-us. They may begin to resonate deeply with the apostle Paul's vision that God will one day "be all and in all" (1 Corinthians 15:28). These disciples are more inclined than most to transcend barriers of doctrine, class, and religious style out of a readiness to experience the unity of God and humanity.

Most older adults, however, need to strengthen the foundations of faith laid in childhood and younger adult years. They may wrestle with guilt over unfinished or inadequately completed work. Certain vital personal relationships may need repair. Sometimes forgiveness must be sought without the possibility of reconciliation, particularly with deceased parents or an estranged spouse.

They may review their spiritual journey, relationships, and contributions to the world and feel unfulfilled. As they face their own mortality, they may also be dealing with aging and dying parents and peers. The role of faith in issues of life and death, as well as questions about life beyond death, becomes particularly significant. They seek wisdom and often have much to offer both their peers and those younger than themselves.

Mature Adults (Ages 70 and Older)

This group of adult Christians can be among the most dedicated and insightful of students. They have both the time to study and the maturity to perceive the depths of truth in the material they work with. As spiritual friends, they bring a lifetime of experience out of which to share the now well-integrated faith they have lived for many years. They need and deserve intellectual stimulation and the opportunity to share their wisdom with others.

Mature adults may be more ready than others both to live and to die by faith (Philippians 1:21). Some will be reaching toward a "unitive faith" in which they have no more questions and no further doubts (James Fowler). Their faith work is to be with God and in God. Their challenge is to savor life while coping graciously with the limitations imposed on them by aging bodies. They are exercising their faith as they deal with the loss of friends and life partners, limited mobility, and other changes in their ability to participate in the mission and community of the church.

They need the support of those younger than themselves and the companionship of their peers. They struggle with letting go of a more active life. Until now, they may have understood themselves to be valuable to society on the basis of their productivity and ability to contribute in measurable ways to the lives of others. While their physical abilities are diminishing, their spiritual acuity may still be increasing. They need to feel valued and can continue to grow spiritually while nurturing others.

Inasmuch as many mature adults have not worked out their salvation in a consistently deliberate way earlier in life, they may struggle in their late adult years with a haunting sense of inner emptiness, lack of personal fulfillment, grief, and dread of dying. Their previous sense of security in God may be unraveling. They may lose hope and their passion for living healthfully.

When these spiritual issues go unresolved, emotional and physical symptoms of depression frequently surface. Others may repress these aspects of themselves and function at an increasingly superficial level, simply coping with activities of daily living more or less successfully or spending their days in leisure activities.

The old and familiar elements of the faith tradition provide comfort and stability for mature adults who successfully overcome these pitfalls of aging. At the same time, however, failing eyesight and hearing loss may make participating in a group increasingly difficult. Younger class members will want to make an extra effort to speak distinctly. Seating arrangements can be altered so that the hearing impaired can watch the lips and body language of participants and leader. Some find large print study and devotional materials helpful.

Many older adults live alone and rarely receive a hug or a personal visit. Daytime *Class Meetings* held in easily accessible locations allow participants to avoid night driving and climbing stairs. While mature adults frequently recognize the *Class Meeting* as their most important appointment of the week, they may find it difficult to be present on a consistent basis. The *Class Leader* will need to enlist other members in maintaining contact with older adults whose attendance becomes irregular. They can go to the home of the aging, homebound class member for the *daily office,* Love Feast, and the distribution of the communion elements.

Summary: Caring for Adults Over the Life Span

At each stage of life, the individual must grow through change and build toward the goal of personal integrity or perfection in love (Matthew 5:48). The Christian will seek to do this with eyes fixed on Christ "until all of us come to the unity of the faith and of the knowledge of the Son of God, to maturity, to the measure of the full stature of Christ" (Ephesians 4:13; see also Colossians 1:1-28). The work of faith formation is done most successfully within a diverse community under competent and faithful leadership.

Each life stage is built on the previous stages of faith formation. When the work of the prior stage is well executed, the work of the succeeding stage will go relatively smoothly. No one achieves perfection at any stage. Everyone must, from time to time, revisit the work of earlier years to repair damage or restore faulty efforts at building integrity. The astute *Class Leader* will become skilled at helping people recognize the work they need to do and at perceiving how they can help others along the way.

9

Troubleshooting

The group covenant provides the parameters within which the *Class Meeting* functions. The commitment of the members to uphold one another and watch over one another in love unites them, as does their common experience of divine *grace*. The teachings of Jesus and the apostles serve as a ready standard for their relationships with one another and with God. Nevertheless, the dynamics of any group require constant monitoring, evaluation, and care. A number of concerns may surface. Considering these potential hazards in advance will alert and equip you to deal effectively with emerging concerns.

Timing

How can everything be accomplished within the stated time frame?
What if members repeatedly show up late?

Rarely is there enough time to accomplish all that you feel compelled to accomplish, given the stated outline for the *Class Meeting*. Moreover, any need to report an unusual event or an unexpected *grace* will take time away from the formal process of the *reflection* and the study. You must begin the meeting on time and end on time, while maintaining an adequate level of satisfaction on the part of as many of the members as possible.

All members should be able to plan their lives around a well-defined commitment to the group. For this reason, you must serve as timekeeper or appoint a timekeeper from among the members. Notify the group when the ten or fifteen minutes set aside for the *reflection* have been used. Then call time when ten minutes remain in the session, during which the group will move into a time of mutual prayer and commitment to respond to God's Word. By maintaining a disciplined use of the allotted time, most members will learn to appreciate and respect the class schedule.

Extending the Lesson: The only exception to the schedule should be when the entire group grants permission to extend the session. Be aware that it is usually unwise to continue a class session after one member has asked to be excused, inasmuch as that member misses whatever takes place after leaving. This can lead to a breakdown in communication.

When you feel that the study time has been inadequate to convey a particularly relevant point, take the liberty to present that part of the lesson the following week. When personal needs surface during the *reflection* that cannot be adequately addressed within the ten to fifteen minutes allotted, arrange to meet with the needy member outside of class time, possibly with two or three class members present. Many classes create prayer partnerships or spiritual friendships by which members know that a particular individual is praying for them through the week and is available for conversation outside of class. This system of mutual caring relieves some of the potential pressures on the class session itself.

Tardiness: If a member repeatedly arrives late, making a disruptive entrance, assume that this person either has a habit that must be broken or a need to be recognized. Avoid commenting publicly on late arrivals. Proceed as if there had been no interruption. This will usually result in increased compliance.

If the member continues to be late, challenge the behavior outside of class and explain how late arrival distracts both from the benefit the individual gains from participating in the class and from the other members' concentration. Remind the member of the group's commitment to begin and end on time. Encourage punctuality.

If this fails, meet privately with the member to seek out any legitimate reasons for tardiness or underlying needs for affirmation. If modifications in the *Class Meeting* schedule should be considered, attempt to adjust the schedule. If the member needs to meet with a class at another time, attempt to arrange for this.

Trust

How will group members develop the level of trust necessary for sharing at a meaningful level?

Openly discuss the question of developing trust within the class session, preferably in the covenanting session. Clearly define how the *Class Meeting* differs from a support group or a therapeutic group. The purpose of the

Class Meeting is not so much inner healing or personal support as growth in discipleship. Group process will proceed more smoothly if everyone understands that the *Class Meeting* is not the place for telling personal stories or revealing family secrets. Members are to report on the state of their relationship with God and their efforts to follow the rule of discipleship.

Meaningful relationships develop over time. Long-term loyalty and mutual understanding provide security for sharing within a group. Confidentiality is vital. Some personality types are highly relational or empathic. They open themselves easily to others and readily engage in caring for one another. Others are by nature private, reserved, and highly controlled emotionally. They do not wish to be probed or exposed. To be effective, you will need to foster an atmosphere of mutual respect that honors the varying needs and the readiness of members to participate.

Discipline

What if a member fails to keep the covenant or is found engaging in a practice that is clearly contrary to the General Rules? How will the class provide supportive discipline without alienating the member?

The key to this delicate work is an atmosphere of caring and trust based on well-established relationships and mutual loyalty. The integrity of the covenant depends not only on the faithfulness and gentleness of all the members, but also on the responsibility of members to monitor their own faithfulness. We are to hold ourselves accountable to God in all humility and avoid condemning others for whom Christ gave his life (Matthew 7:1-5; Romans 2:1; 8:1). Your class members must not expect one another to have arrived at perfection; each must have a continuing desire to grow more like Christ day by day, with the goal of reaching toward perfection in love. Members demonstrate their faithfulness by showing mercy and doing all in their power to uphold the weak or troubled in a spirit of gentleness. At the same time, members have a fundamental obligation to one another to warn one another against the dangers of abridging scriptural holiness (Leviticus 19:17-18; 2 Thessalonians 3:15; Colossians 3:16).

First Thessalonians 5:12-24 and Matthew 18:15-20 provide vital instruction for leaders and members who struggle with matters of community discipline. The first principle is that as *Class Leader* you must take the responsibility of oversight, as a pastoral person. The members are to come to respect the office of *Class Leader* as that of an overseer of souls charged with maintaining the integrity of the faith community. Second, the members are to consider it their covenant responsibility to one another to uphold the standards that the members have agreed upon in light of their common call to follow Christ. They are to challenge, admonish, instruct, and encourage one another in so doing. All matters of discipline must be handled with prayer, respect for the dignity of the member in question, compassion, and appropriate privacy.

The least inflammatory means of addressing the problem is always the preferable one. When members isolate themselves from the class by missing a meeting or refusing to speak openly and honestly, either within the formal *reflection* or during a more private conversation, every effort should be made to reach out in compassion to nurture the faith and trust of the straying members. In the end, however, the goal of true repentance and holiness of heart and life must be preserved. Both are essential to the well-being of the entire class, as well as the individual member. To relax the standards of discipline is to yield to disorder and fruitless religion. In other words, the responsibility for discipline among the class members belongs first to the individual, then to you as *Class Leader* and, finally, to the class as a whole.

Privacy

What if a member feels violated by the reflection?

Since Methodists have lost any expectation of being examined and held accountable to a standard of behavior and religious practice, long-time Methodists may take issue with this key component of the system of discipleship. One member reported that she initially found the Wesleyan question, "How is it with your soul?" strange, invasive, and offensive. She had certainly never been asked that question before. Some consider the practice of confessing one's sins and failures a Roman Catholic practice outmoded by the Protestant doctrine of justification by *grace* through faith. The *Class Leader* has a teaching role in responding to any reluctance on the part of members to participate in the *reflection*.

While members may choose to remain silent or say very little during the *reflection* on a given week, if this pattern persists, speak privately with them to question why they are responding in this way. Some modification in the method of the *reflection* may be advisable. Encourage all members to contribute to an ongoing evaluation of their class process.

At the end of the first five or six weeks, devote a full thirty minutes of the class session to hearing from every member regarding their experience of the class, how it has been helpful and what aspect of it has been less than helpful. Changes can be made in light of group preferences, as long as the foundational intent of the *Class Meeting* is preserved. Anyone who expresses concern should be respected and know that their concerns will be integrated into the process of evaluation. All members should have a part in determining the future of the group. The culture of their particular *Class Meeting* should reflect the preferences of its membership. Your queries and the responses of the members should both respect the privacy of those who participate and honor the purpose of the *Class Meeting*.

On the other hand, some people object to the *reflection* because it requires something of them that they are not ready to give or exposes something that they wish to keep hidden. The individualism of Western society fosters pride and independence. It ignores the truth that the integrity of any community depends on the wholeness of each of its members. What one does in secret ultimately affects everyone in some way. It is not only for the benefit of the individual that Methodists engage in mutual examination, but for the sake of the kingdom of God and the honor due God's name. All Christians need to be encouraged to seek to become like Christ, lest they lead some astray or bring dishonor to the gospel (Matthew 5:13-20).

Resistance

What if my group isn't ready for this? Suppose I find that they are unwilling to spend time sharing their spiritual lives with one another or are unwilling to engage in a daily prayer life? What if a member doesn't yet attend church regularly?

As a *Class Leader*, you may have to step back from your original plan and recognize that your role is to reach out to meet people where they are. Build a relationship of caring trust with the people you serve. They may then allow you to relate them to God and nurture them in the faith.

You may be unable to form a *Class Meeting* as soon as you had hoped. It is better to delay the formation of a class than to deform the intention of the *Class Meeting* to satisfy the needs and desires of people who are not yet receptive. If, on the other hand, you feel resistance from one person or a minority within the class, do not allow the resistance to distract the progress of the majority.

It is always wise to explore the resistance, both within the class session and then in private with the individuals concerned. Often the resistance is not what it appears to be. Frequently, when it is clarified, it can be addressed in a mutually satisfactory way. For example, you might be using a format for the *reflection*, daily prayer, or study that is not well suited to the interests and abilities of some of the members. With fuller insight into the problem at hand, including knowledge of the personalities and learning styles of those who pose resistance, you may be able to plan *Class Meetings* that benefit everyone.

Domineering Behavior

How should I respond to a member who tends to monopolize group time or dominate conversation?

Inevitably you will find yourself in the position of wondering how best to deal with a disruptive, controlling, or dominant personality. An equally serious challenge comes from passive-aggressive behavior patterns. First, identify the problem before it becomes a serious impediment to group process. Then address the concern openly in the group as a matter of general concern. Ask everyone to take responsibility for monitoring their own behavior and helping to manage the group process. If necessary, redirect the class by interrupting the dominant or disruptive member.

Teach active listening skills both by modeling them and by providing instructional time on this vital skill. Review the procedure of the *Class Meeting*, reinforcing the need for brevity and preparedness. Remind members to speak concisely and report forthrightly on the state of their souls. They are to offer carefully thought-out questions or comments for study and *reflection*, preferably prepared before class.

The next level of approach to the problem is to speak privately with the individual in question. He or she may be misinterpreting the culture of the Wesleyan *Class Meeting*, based on prior experience with a support group or other therapeutic process. It is unfair to the other members to allow one member to destroy the effectiveness of the class.

Diversion

What if members are so needy they want to use the Class Meeting *for personal therapy or problem solving?*

The pattern must be addressed promptly, lest the purpose of the *Class Meeting* be distorted. More often than not, the needy person will benefit from individual contact from you or another spiritual friend from within the group. If the behavior recurs after the initial problem resolves itself, you may need to review within the class session the differences among support groups, group counseling sessions, prayer meetings, and *Class Meeting*s. The primary task of the *Class Meeting* is to encourage growth in Christian discipleship among the members.

Conflict

What should I do when two or more members become involved in an interpersonal conflict?

Read Philippians 2:1-16; 4:2-3. Lead a study on these passages, followed by worship, including confession and the passing of the peace. Pray for one another. In this way, the members apply the wisdom and experience of the church to their own circumstance and correct themselves in light of their longing to bring their behavior into conformity with the aims of the gospel.

If this does not resolve the conflict, meet privately with the parties involved and attempt to serve as a mediator. Make them aware that their relationship and their conflict are important to the church and affect the unity of the Body of Christ. From beginning to end, pray for all parties concerned. Exercise discernment, recognizing that the conflict may be symptomatic of more serious issues that need to be addressed by a pastor. Confer with the pastor in charge.

Group "Dis-ease"

What if the group becomes unhealthy? Suppose study or failure in fulfilling the covenant leads to a crisis of faith, perfectionist guilt, or discouragement on the part of more than one member. What if attendance declines?

Identify the source of stress and diagnose the problem. Following the diagnosis, with the oversight of the pastor or coordinator, develop a case-specific treatment plan.

1. Ask the members what they are thinking and feeling, offer feedback, and seek clarification or further information.
2. Engage the members in brainstorming about how to address their concerns.
3. Pray for everyone involved. Listen for the Word of God. Seek discernment.

4. Review the information and proposals with the coordinator or pastor and the *band*.
5. Develop and implement a strategy for restoring group health.

(Note: Take care to recognize hidden agendas, unspoken concerns, and efforts to save face or protect the feelings of a member or you as *Class Leader*. All too often, when the real issue has not been named, leaders attempt premature solutions but fail to resolve the dis-ease. Often some significant change is needed, such as retraining the leader, changing leadership, or disbanding and reorganizing.)

Syncretism

What if spiritual practices surface that cannot legitimately be used within the structure of the Wesleyan Class Meeting *system?*

Honor the intent and faith of the person for whom the practice in question seems helpful and minimize any attention given to it within the class session. More than likely, as the individual gains spiritual strength from keeping the covenant and participating in the *Class Meeting*, as well as from public worship with the congregation, these incompatible practices will become less significant. On the other hand, they may have become a part of the member's practice in formative years and have deep and lasting emotional significance for him or her. These religious practices may continue to be valuable to the member personally, even when imposing them on the *Class Meeting* may be inappropriate. For guidance in these matters, refer to Paul's discussion of the strong honoring the weak for the good of all (Romans 14:1–15:2). Paul writes, "Welcome those who are weak in faith, but not for the purpose of quarreling over opinions. . . . We who are strong ought to put up with the failings of the weak, and not to please ourselves. Each of us must please our neighbor for the good purpose of building up the neighbor" (Romans 14:1; 15:1-2).

Mental Illness or Personal Crisis

How should a class care for a member who is not well? What happens if I am in a time of personal crisis?

112

Class members who become victims of depression or any other serious emotional disability may not be able to maintain faithful observance of the class covenant. They may feel guilty, ashamed, inferior, or unable to talk about the state of their souls without breaking down. For any of these reasons, the member may drop away from the class.

A person suffering from some acute personal stress may, on the other hand, divert the process of the *Class Meeting*, transforming it into something of a self-help session. Identify the problem and seek help for the member in another context. Report your concerns to the pastor in charge.

Tragically, depression and other forms of mental illness leave Christians unable to feel the presence of God. They find themselves less able to absorb new material. Depression diminishes tolerance for social interaction. Persons suffering from depression may find themselves irritable, dispassionate, or disengaged. In addition, they may weep easily, experience insomnia, and find their daily routines interrupted. Patterns of pervasive shame and guilt are common. For all these reasons, normal participation in the life of the class may be diminished.

Persons suffering in these ways need care, but they may resist it. Uphold these members in prayer and offer personal support without becoming inappropriately engaged in caregiving. Sometimes the best way to reach out is through cards and letters. When such a member misses a class, contact from another member may provide a vital link with God and with life itself. Watch for any signs of members becoming overly responsible, however, for the well-being of fellow class members and report such a potential problem to the pastor in charge.

The reality of congregational life is that people who have chronic emotional needs find the church a less judgmental and more supportive environment than most others. Any small group setting provides much needed opportunities for friendship and caring. For this reason, people who live with mental illness gravitate to *Class Meetings*. It is not uncommon for half of the members of a class to suffer from depression or other manifestations of chronic stress. Seek continuing education and supervision in dealing with this pervasive problem, in order to meet the needs of class members effectively while focusing on fostering growth in Christian discipleship.

If you experience a significant personal crisis, take a leave of absence. During such a leave, continue to function, whenever possible, as a member of the *band*. When appropriate, seek professional help and remain under the care of the pastor in charge.

Burnout

How do I know when it's time to resign?

Evaluate yourself by looking for any of the following warning signs:

Category One: Primary Effectiveness

1. *Loss of passion* regarding the nurturing of disciples
2. *Loss of compassion* for class members
3. *Loss of commitment* to personal spiritual, moral, and missional disciplines

Category Two: Secondary Effectiveness

1. *Loss of vision* regarding the kingdom of God in the midst of the people and the class members' potential for maturing into the likeness of Christ
2. *Weariness*
3. *Sense of failure* or inadequacy
4. *Unresolved conflict*
5. *Sustained decline* in class participation

When a Category One symptom occurs, immediately report this to the coordinator and share it with the *band*. When any of the five symptoms in Category Two occurs, in addition to one of the Category One symptoms, consider asking for a leave of absence and consult with the pastor and coordinator. When more than two of the symptoms in the first category and more than two from the second category occur, consult with the pastor and consider resigning. Note that as long as qualities necessary for primary effectiveness are in place, matters related to secondary effectiveness can be managed with the support of the pastor, *director*, and *band*, when supplemented by continuing education and other stress-management strategies.

1 0

Caring for the Class Over
Its Life Cycle

Just as individuals grow and change over their life span, so small groups move through relatively predictable stages. Thus far, we have focused on the first year during which the group is conceived, formed, and guided into stability and effectiveness. The initiation phase of the *Class Meeting* system and the birthing process for any new class has its own challenges. Later phases need equal attention. Guiding a group through the later phases requires keen insight and strategic responses to emerging issues.

Several phases of group life can be anticipated:

1. Initiation
2. Growth and productivity
3. Resistance
4. Conflict
5. Alienation and change
6. Shifts in group dynamics or leadership
7. Renewal or decline
8. Closure

Assess where your class is in its life span and address its particular needs. In order to accurately diagnose the problems that inevitably occur and then treat them effectively, seek to understand the characteristics of each phase of group life. A variety of effective approaches to managing change apply to various phases of any group's life cycle. The challenge is, of course, to choose the right approach and to employ it appropriately. Doing so will enhance the effectiveness of the system, limit the guilt and sense of failure that leaders often feel, and equip everyone to adjust responsibly.

The class will probably enjoy a long season of growth in discipleship, assuming that the initiation phase fostered a strong sense of mutual respect and loyalty among the members, a clearly understood set of core values and group norms, and good listening skills. The class will be fulfilling for its members and will naturally renew itself over time. The class will be well positioned to contribute to the larger community of faith.

Addressing Issues During Growth and Productivity

Important potential concerns during the second phase of the group's life cycle (possibly the most productive period in what will become the history of the class), include:

- Laxity

- Breaking covenant

- Diverse needs and agenda among group members

- Conflicts

- Disenchantment

- Elitism

- Group closure

- Imbalance

Laxity

Address any lack of discipline through the *reflection*. This approach encourages members to confess voluntarily their struggle to remain faithful and allows the class members to offer encouragement. In this way, the members demonstrate an internal desire to grow in faithfulness and the covenant is preserved without offense to anyone. Members thus avoid feeling that the covenant is a restrictive rule; instead, they see the covenant as a genuine means of support. When you detect some dishonesty or avoidance on the part of a member, speak to the member privately in a nonjudging and nurturing spirit. This private counsel may expose needs that require a deeper level of care. Confer with the pastor in charge.

Breaking Covenant

Groups often violate their own process. One of the most common infractions is meeting beyond the stated time frame. You will frequently want to wait until all members have arrived to begin the session. By doing so, you violate the faithfulness and the expectations of those who arrive on time. These and other small infractions can lead to alienation. Guard against occasions for conflict by regularly reviewing the covenant, honoring it, recognizing the discomfort of members, and accepting feedback nondefensively.

Diverse Needs and Agenda

All of us bring our own vision and motivations for faithful discipleship. At the same time, we lack full self-awareness regarding our personality traits, interpersonal skills, and subconscious or preconscious needs. Nevertheless, all of these things affect group dynamics. Watch and listen for signs of the many levels at which individuals function within the group, discuss these confidentially with peers, and facilitate classes so that group members assist each other toward fuller self-awareness and gracious conflict resolution.

Conflicts

One of the highest priorities of Christian community is to preserve the bond of fellowship. We do this by working for peace in light of a covenant of mutual forgiveness. We deliberately break patterns of accusing, blaming, shaming, denial, and avoidance. Good leaders encourage members to agree to follow the difficult path of going to their brother or sister in private and in love to seek reconciliation before taking any conflict to a higher level or discussing the matter with a third party. Christian faithfulness precludes gossip or speaking about the person with others before confronting the issue directly and discreetly.

When personality conflicts surface in a group, empower the members to care for one another openly in the context of the *Class Meeting* or guide members to speak privately, but directly, honestly, and in a nonjudging way to the parties involved. Conflicts within a group sometimes require interrupting the usual format of the class for a time of silence or prayer. Resolving a conflict and facilitating progress in any class session may necessitate setting aside part of the group's regular agenda for that day.

Disenchantment

Disenchantment with the *Class Meeting* system may develop as a result of boredom, personality conflicts, or poor management of the covenant. Sometimes, however, people become dissatisfied as a result of matters wholly unrelated to the class itself. When evidence of disenchantment surfaces, you must take care to identify the signs and seek clarification of the issues before the problem leads to disengagement on the part of one or more members.

If someone becomes restless with the format of the class, demonstrate genuine openness to creative feedback. Accept criticism gracefully and assume that members intend to be helpful. Engage them in developing creative solutions. Consult this manual for models and approaches that will refresh the process of the *Class Meeting* and honor the diverse and changing needs of different personalities or life stages. Consult the *director* of the classes or the pastor in charge. By all means, acknowledge the problem and validate the member or members who express themselves. At the same time, avoid diverting the class from its stated mission or modifying the methodology of the class to such an extent that the changes dilute the impact of the discipleship system.

Elitism

One of the dangers of forming *Class Meetings* within a larger and already established Christian community is the potential for divisiveness. Class members can begin to consider themselves better Christians than those who do not participate in a class. On the other hand, nonparticipants may feel inferior and defensive. They may also perceive that Class Members consider themselves an elite group.

Great care must be taken to avoid this set of damaging dynamics. First, your church should provide alternative approaches to accountable discipleship. Second, communicate through several means as often as possible about the openness of the *Class Meeting* system and how to become a part of it. Third, honor the faithfulness of people who express their discipleship through other means. Prepare the entire congregation for the potential for elitism and explain how the church plans to avoid this problem.

Group Closure

In a settled culture, where people spend their entire lifetimes in one neighborhood and remain members of the same church from birth through death, the class one joins upon confirmation or conversion is the class one remains a part of for many years. Such a class welcomes new people only as members die or drift away. In North America, however, many people move every few years. For this reason, healthy churches design their discipleship systems to accommodate frequent changes in membership.

Because trust develops over time in the context of meaningful relationships and because every group develops its own culture and norms, most classes tend to become uncomfortable with integrating newcomers or guests on a casual basis. Doing so limits the intimacy of the class and fosters reserve in confession and faith-sharing. Frequently, the confidentiality and trust developed within a class necessitates closing the group to potential newcomers in order to protect the growth process of the members.

For these reasons, it is best to determine in advance how your class will define its mission. Will it organize itself with the intention of remaining open to newcomers, accepting the necessary disadvantages and recognizing the need to welcome newcomers intentionally? Or will it plan for closure? If the group chooses to close its membership, it will also need to plan for regular reorganization. Reorganizing will allow members to move or otherwise leave graciously. It will also facilitate integrating new people or splitting to form a new class. Most midsize congregations should plan for both closed and open *Class Meetings*. Larger churches will generally prefer to start new classes on a frequent basis and guide all new disciples into newly forming classes.

Imbalance

Every class develops its own personality. Like individuals, a particular group may become more introspective or more extroverted, more reflective than active, or more active than reflective. Group health depends on your commitment to seeking healthy balance in the life of the class.

Just as introspective people must honor their need for quiet, solitude, meditation, study, and intellectual stimulation, while complementing their spiritual practices with service and interaction with others, group health depends on balancing and enriching itself with experiences it might not naturally choose. One way of ensuring this is to vary the study materials the group uses on a quarterly basis, in order to incorporate Bible study, spirituality, social justice issues, and missions into the curriculum over the course of each year.

An alternative is to engage members in an action/reflection model of service learning. Under this model, your class would study for a stated period of time and then engage in a mission project. After completing the project, your class would evaluate its experience and begin a new cycle. An alternative application of the action/reflection model is to agree that members will work on individual mission projects outside of class and reflect on them within class time, in light of a course of study or in the context of the *reflection*.

During class sessions, members consider how effectively they practiced their faith and fulfilled the mission of Christ while serving. If, on the other hand, the class is fundamentally an administrative body or a ministry team, health and balance can be achieved by retreating for spiritual renewal. Consider holding a quarterly meeting for covenant renewal and spiritual enrichment. In any case, you assume the pastoral function of assessing the health of your class, fostering enrichment, encouraging experimentation, and developing group self-awareness.

When Resistance Surfaces

After the organizational phase and a season of productivity and spiritual growth, an uncomfortable set of symptoms may begin to appear. Signs of resistance include spotty attendance without checking in. Shallow or evasive responses during the *reflection* may indicate discomfort with the process. Passive behavior, including silence or nonverbal indications of distress, should also be explored.

Listen actively for unspoken needs behind verbal challenges regarding the practice of the group. Seek clarification and feedback. In other words, deal with symptoms of resistance early, before they get out of control. Recognize that the symptom may mask the real issue. Unless you are proactive in dealing with resistance, your class may not survive.

Determine how and when to address resistance effectively. Know the temperaments and circumstances of the individuals involved and assess the depth of their discipleship. Seek the best way both to minimize conflict and expose underlying problems, while preserving the group process. Avoid allowing one or two people's resistance to undermine the effectiveness of the experience for the majority. Note, however, that resistance expressed by one often echoes the otherwise unexpressed needs and concerns of others. Some persons are less able or willing to disguise their difficulties with the process of the group.

Obviously, you or the class itself must not only hear but also respond to the concerns of members. It will be impossible, however, to please everyone and inadvisable to try to do so over the long term. When a member's resistance cannot be resolved and that person chooses to leave the class, acknowledge a sense of loss, lead the class in meaningful grieving, and, wherever possible, facilitate closure within the group. If possible, involve the departing member in a time of reconciliation or healing. Because class members have entered into a sacred covenant and build meaningful friendships, all efforts should be made to create a level of loyalty that requires anyone who leaves the group to do so in a gracious and somewhat formal manner, thereby honoring the covenantal relationship.

When Intragroup Conflict Occurs

When members invest deeply in a covenantal way of life and find in it something vital to their faith and personal well-being, they sometimes find themselves fighting to preserve the process or values of their group. Simply because they are unique individuals, they will disagree with one another from time to time. Expect conflict and prepare to manage it by way of continuing education and support from the coordinator and other *Class Leaders*.

Effective conflict resolution within a Wesleyan *Class Meeting* begins with respect for all parties and a commitment to keep the focus of the group on their common vision and mission. The leader expects that all parties value becoming more like Jesus and fulfilling God's saving purpose above everything else. Keep this goal before the conflicted parties while mediating the conflict.

When the conflict is between you and one or more members, however, avoid allowing the conflict to become personal or presuming that you understand the problem before thoroughly investigating it. Carefully identify the issue and seek to deal with it objectively. Speak with one another in terms of personal feelings, needs, and hopes. Avoid accusatory language or a judging attitude of superiority. Model mutual loyalty by disagreeing in love, and seek a healthy resolution of issues through open, honest conflict resolution. Remember the wisdom of John Wesley's principle for preserving a catholic spirit: "In essentials unity; in nonessentials freedom; in all things love." Pray with the party involved.

Trust that conflict can serve the common good and lead to growth in character and group effectiveness. Peace is not the absence of conflict. It is, instead, a dynamic process of love in action. Disagreeing in love can be a necessary phase of enabling a sacred and creative process of change.

Change or Stagnation

Regular evaluation helps to preserve the health of any class or team. When a group engages in corporate self-examination, it avoids stagnation and fosters its own development. Some groups benefit from evaluation every six to eight weeks. Others prefer to recovenant quarterly or annually. A well-organized *Class Meeting* system includes a plan for different aspects of evaluation at several points each year.

In the formative phase, your class should evaluate all aspects of its life after the initial five or six meetings to perfect the covenant for long-term use. Groups typically learn quickly what works best for them. Minor changes can be made easily as the need arises.

After each quarter of the year, your class should evaluate its primary focus and effectiveness in meeting its goals. In many classes, this programmatic evaluation will focus on curriculum and the format for study. Ministry teams that are also functioning as Wesleyan *Class Meetings* will evaluate the work being done by the members and engage in quarterly or midrange planning.

Evaluate, celebrate, or change leadership on an annual basis. You may be gifted at filling a supporting role, such as administration or teaching, rather than leading a class. Avoid leadership burnout by shifting responsibilities. Honesty in these matters may vastly extend the life span of your class. Like all *Class Leaders*, you will need continuing education for leadership skill development. The evaluation process may serve to identify specific skills that you should seek to gain over the coming year.

At each stage of *reflection*, healthy classes hold themselves accountable to scriptural models of Christian community under the authority of Christ. New Testament resources for group *reflection* on the maintenance of discipline and conflict resolution include: Matthew 5:21-26; 7:1-5, 12; 18:15-22; Luke 17:1-4; Romans 12:1-18; 14:10-19; Galatians 6:1-10; Ephesians 4:1-16; and James 5:19-20. Your *Class Meetings* should be an experiment in Christian living. Understand the *Class Meeting* as a laboratory for realizing Jesus' vision: "Repent, for the kingdom of heaven has come near" (Matthew 4:17).

When Differences Result in Alienation and Loss

Even the most diligent exercise of evaluation and change management, including negotiating disputes and applying biblical conflict resolution strategies, cannot protect the church against a member's conclusion that leaving the class is healthier than staying. Just as forgiveness does not always lead to reconciliation, so also some differences cannot be resolved except through distancing. Sometimes a member must leave to tend to personal matters in a separate context. Private counseling or a change of *Class Meeting* may lead to healing and a return to a covenantal relationship within the Wesleyan *Class Meeting* system. Ideally, the door remains open for return and members preserve an atmosphere in which returning can be both wise and caring for all parties.

Classes base their membership on observing an objective standard of discipleship, but in reality, the subjective elements of belonging play an equally important role in determining who will participate and for how long. People choose to belong because they feel accepted, valued, and cared for. They stay as long as they can identify with at least one other member of the group, and feel comfortable with the core values and traditions of the group. Long-term members share a similar vision and level of dedication. As long as these factors remain in place, the causes for alienation are usually related to:

• Personality conflict

• Leadership style

• Emotional instability

• Personal crisis

Sometimes members leave because of a loss of faith or inability to keep the covenant, but give other reasons. Often people who are alienated project their own unresolved issues onto the group or its leader.

Accurately identifying the cause of alienation can contribute significantly to healthy grieving and growth when a member leaves. Ideally, all parties will feel responsible at some level and will learn from the experience. This allows them to communicate clearly and part with a sense of mutual blessing and forgiveness.

Graceful Change

Both when a member leaves and when a new leader or new member enters, group dynamics change. A period of reorientation ensues. This necessarily involves getting acquainted, building trust, and adjusting to a new set of personalities. It may involve a change of format for the *Class Meeting*. It usually implies emphasizing relationships over study or service, at least during the initial meeting. Never prefer the group's perceived task over relationship building.

When new people come and go frequently, determine the group's tolerance for emphasizing hospitality over its other functions. Sensitivity and caring for people's unspoken needs, active listening, and seeking clarification, combined with tolerance and patience, will prove to be your best tools of leadership in the midst of change. Particularly when the newcomer is already well known, has excellent social skills, or prefers to enter a group slowly and quietly, relationship building and other aspects of orienting newcomers can be handled outside the regular *Class Meeting*. Your group's prior experience, personality dynamics, and cultural norms will determine what approaches will be most effective in encouraging newcomers to be open and self-revealing.

Fostering Renewal and Delaying Decline

Several tools for group renewal can transform unavoidable changes over the life span of any group into experiences of divine *grace*. Just as individuals at midlife often benefit from spiritual guidance, mature groups can develop under the skilled direction of a retreat leader or consultant. In a retreat setting, members can look back on corporate aging and grieving, as well as times of growth and insight, and value them as periods of being carried by God. Seasons of desolation, if and when they are given a biblical frame of reference, can be seen as sojourns in a sacred wilderness, rather than as disabling loss. Groups can find renewal by seeing their life together from a faith perspective. Renewal can occur as surely as spring follows winter.

The Love Feast can also provide a change of format and bring new energy to your *Class Meeting*. A holy quiet cleanses the souls of the members as they sing spiritual songs, participate in spontaneous praise and thanksgiving, testify to God's *grace,* and pray for one another around a simple meal. Joy, peace, and renewed righteousness replace boredom and dissatisfaction. God's love is once again "spread abroad" in the hearts of the believers (Romans 5:5).

When It Is Time to Disband

A wide range of factors can lead to the death of a class or other small group within the church:

1. Loss of vision, mission, discipline, faith, leadership, or members
2. Completion of a stated mission
3. Conflict or crisis
4. Aging of members
5. Failure to maintain and renew the group
6. Unskilled leadership
7. Lack of supervision
8. An outmoded covenant and group culture

While careful leadership can prolong the life of any group, all classes lose their vitality at some point. The question becomes, *How shall we respect the past, honor those who kept covenant and lived faithfully, and celebrate the fruits of this ministry, in order to move on to a fresh expression of Christian discipleship?*

A number of approaches have been taken to dissolve a covenant group. The worst are to be avoided at all cost: disappearing, blaming, or refusing to let the group die with dignity. People may drop out without explaining themselves, or express their disappointment and alienation by criticizing the group or its leader. In some cases, groups employ manipulative or deceitful methods to recruit or retain members in a desperate attempt to keep a group alive, long after its useful life has ended. In so doing, they violate the integrity of the *Class Meeting* and its original purpose. These approaches reflect unhealthy grieving.

Mature and responsible leaders anticipate the time to disband and prepare for it as one would the end of any important relationship. They tell the group's story, express appreciation, and celebrate the group's work. Members take time out from group work to reassess their own needs, gifts, skills, availability, and responsibility in relation to Christ. They wonder how to help give birth to a new setting for accountable discipleship and actively seek an alternative approach to faithfulness for themselves. They find ways of supporting others who sincerely desire to follow Christ. Creative approaches to disbanding a class integrate the best of the past so as to bequeath this heritage to a new generation of *Class Meetings*.

A Prayer for All Who Seek Discipleship Through Class Meetings

Spirit of God: Quicken our souls as on a new resurrection morning. Raise us from the past to live the hope of the gospel anew. Transform our ordinary communities into sacred places where God is visible and available for all. Fill us with such love and divine vision that others may receive the life once revealed in Jesus of Nazareth, in whose name we live and pray. Amen.

Glossary

Accountability Group: A small group or community pledged to participate in defined spiritual disciplines. The group meets on a regular basis to answer to one another with respect to the degree to which members have engaged in the spiritual disciplines. The group also questions its members about individual growth in faith and personal experience of spiritual life. The conversation in which members give account of themselves is defined as *Christian Conferencing.* (See also *reflection.*)

Anthropomorphic: Having human characteristics.

Anthropomorphism: Attributing human characteristics to God.

Band: A unit of Methodist *Class Leaders* or other lay ministers who meet with a *minister* or *director* who oversees their souls and their work.

Band leader: Usually the *minister* in charge, also referred to as the *director.*

Class Leader: A mature Christian, not recently converted, who demonstrates pastoral abilities for the care of souls, speaks fluently, listens actively and with patience, has a command of the Bible, Methodist teaching and organizational structure, and has been trained and commissioned for the office of *Class Leader* in a Methodist church.

Class Meeting: A unit of twelve laypeople who have been converted to Christ and organized to pursue holiness of heart and life, following a common rule of life and meeting weekly with a *Class Leader* to hold one another accountable, "watching over one another in love," originally, those who "earnestly desire to flee from the wrath to come."

Christian Conferencing: Conversation among disciples of Christ with the goal of seeking "the mind of Christ" relative to matters of faith and practice.

Connection: The Methodist system for making disciples of converts and maintaining lifelong faithfulness among its members through the annual conference, the quarterly conference, the *society* meeting or congregational worship and prayer meetings, and the *Class Meeting.*

Covenant Service: An order of worship designed by John Wesley to be used annually near the beginning of the new year by all Methodists for the purpose of renewing commitment to serve God and pursue holiness of heart and life.

Daily office: A guide to prayer to be used each day of the week, whether alone or with an assembly of believers; usually as derived from the order prescribed in the *Book of Common Prayer.*

Director: The leader of the *band* of *Class Leaders.*

Epistle: New Testament writings excluding the four Gospels.

Forms of prayer: Written prayers for various purposes.

General Rules: The three-part community discipline that John Wesley developed for Methodists and published in 1743.

Grace: The gift of God to humanity for the purpose of its salvation from sin and death; God's saving work as revealed in Jesus, his death and resurrection, that results in a change of heart and life whereby the believer can love God with heart, soul, mind, and strength, and the neighbor as the self. (Note: Faith is a gift [*grace*] of God and not an act of will, though it involves responding to God with reason, feeling, affection, and awe.)

Instituted means of grace: The practices that tend to enhance one's love for God and neighbor; those forms in which Jesus engaged or taught his disciples to use in relating to God; the sacraments of Holy Communion and Baptism, prayer, public worship, fasting or abstinence, searching the Scriptures, and *Christian Conferencing.*

Lay assistant: An unordained but identified leader among the members who extends the reach of the ordained clergy in the work of pastoral care or the oversight of souls, frequently including matters of financial stewardship or the management of the organization's temporal affairs.

Lectio divina: "Sacred reading," either of scripture or of devotional literature for the purpose of listening for the Word of God.

Minister: The pastor in charge, often serving as the *band leader* but only rarely as *Class Leader.*

Ordinances of God: The means of *grace* instituted by Christ and recognized by the church.

Prayer for Illumination: An act of petition in which the supplicant asks God to enlighten the minds and hearts of the hearers as the Scriptures are read and God's Word proclaimed; a prayer that precedes the reading and study of Scripture in the *Class Meeting* or other gathering of Methodists.

Prevenient grace (also **preventing grace**)**:** The work of God that comes before conversion; God's love at work in the lives of all human beings, well before they are aware of God's *grace* or seek after it; God's *grace* preventing people from falling into eternal damnation by drawing them toward God and a right way of living in relationship with God and neighbor. (Note: God's *prevenient grace* can be resisted.)

Prudential means of grace: Those practices that common sense indicates serve to build up the Body of Christ and that experience has proved to be fruitful in so doing; the *Class Meeting*, the *society* meeting, the annual conference, the Quarterly Meeting, and family prayer.

Reflection: A means of maintaining accountability to the rule of life appropriate to a disciple of Jesus Christ, usually practiced in private, preferably at the close of the day, and in the *Class Meeting*, as a form of confession; based on the objective standard of the *General Rules*, the Scriptures of the Old and New Testaments, and the teachings and example of Jesus.

Society: A religious association; originally a midweek gathering of Methodists in good standing with their *Class Meetings*, as certified by their *Class Leader* or the *minister*.

Syncretism: The amalgamation of different religions, cultures, or schools of thought.

I